THESE ALSO **PRAYED**

A YEAR OF PRAYER THOUGHTS FROM AUTHORS YOU MAY OR MAY NOT KNOW

Compiled by
DAN R. CRAWFORD

7710-T Cherry Park Drive, Ste 224

Houston, TX 77095

713-766-4271

www.WorldwidePublishingGroup.com

ISBN: 978-1-0879-9319-5

CONTENTS

ENDORSEMENTS

"Dr. Dan Crawford has been studying, pondering, teaching, preaching, and writing on prayer for a long time! He knows the subject as well as anyone I know. In this new book you'll gain the benefit of his years of careful study as he shares inspiring nuggets on the crucial practice of prayer."

> **Dr. Richard Blackaby, President**, Blackaby Ministries International, co-author, *Experiencing God"*

"Dr. Dan Crawford has put together a wonderful resource on prayer quotes that can be used in teaching, sermons, as well as food for thought in one's own personal prayer life. Though there are many trends in ministry that come and go, the necessity and relevance of prayer stays the same. You will be encouraged to strengthen your personal and cooperate prayer life and desire to know the heart of the Father more intimately through this book."

> **Dr. Cathie Smith**, Ministry Wives Coordinator, *Great Commission Association of Southern Baptist Churches,* California; Former missionary to Spain; Author of, *In His Grip: A Divine Weaving of Faith, Circumstance, Community & Prayer*

"For many years I have read the books Dan Crawford has produced. They have challenged me and taught me many truths of the Bible. They have been a source for numerous Bible studies and sermons. I am glad he has produced another one."

> **Lynn Sasser**, Pastor, *Capital City Baptist Church*, Mexico City, Mexico

"No discipline connects believers directly to the heart of God as the discipline of prayer. Through the ages, writers have recorded gems of wisdom that teach believers about prayer. In the years of ministry and of teaching prayer, Dr. Crawford has discovered many of these gems that have in turn shaped his prayer life as well as the prayer lives of his students. In this book, he shares some of the gems of wisdom about prayer that will help to shape an even deeper prayer experience for the reader - gems of wisdom that might be lost in this day were it not for a volume like this one."

> **Dr. Evelyn Joyce Ashcraft**, Associate State Director, *Texas Baptist Student Ministry*, Retired, Baptist General Convention of Texas

"A few years ago, I bought a book on the recommendation of a friend entitled, *The Desert Fathers: Sayings of the Early Christian Monks.* I was richly blessed by the sayings of some men and women that many (most?) of us have never heard of. Dr. Crawford has hit a similar note with *These Also Prayed.* These glimpses into the lives of prayer warriors of the past, many of whom we've never read, are a treasure and a blessing. Thanks, Dr. Dan! I'm looking forward to more times of reflection, of refreshment, and of challenge through these voices from the past."

> **Steve Seaberry**, Chaplain, *Dakar Academy*, Dakar, Senegal, West Africa

"I have been blessed for over forty years by Dr. Dan Crawford's focus on the importance of prayer in the life of every believer, and that was simply confirmed to me during thirty years on the mission field. Our ever-growing relationship with our Father God is what enables us to pray audacious prayers and believe He will answer us in the best way possible. I am sure this book of quotes from a wide spectrum of authors will not only bless the reader, but also expand that person's understanding of the purpose and life-giving importance of prayer."

> **Patricia Wilkendorf**, Member Care Resource Coordinator, *Wycliffe Bible Translators*; Former Translation Consultant at SIL International, Yaoundé, Cameroon

"I have known the internationally renowned professor and author Dr. Dan Crawford for over twenty years. He is a man of prayer, who writes and speaks out of personal experience. Through this book, he encourages readers to pray daily and shares deep insights and truths about prayer from valuable sources. Whoever reads this book will be inspired in prayer!"

> **Dr. Heinrich Derksen**, President, *Bible Seminary*, Bonn, Germany

"We learn to pray by praying. But sometimes the learning can be moved along by hearing from men and women in the church who have labored in the school prayer with the Spirit of God. Dr. Dan Crawford has gathered up some of those timely lessons for us in *These Also Prayed*."

> **Dr. Craig O'Brien**, Pastor, *Origin Church*, Vancouver, British Columbia, Canada; Coordinating Chaplain University Multi-faith Chaplains Association, University of British Columbia

INTRODUCTION

Over the decades of teaching prayer, I have collected in excess of five hundred books on the subject, plus another two hundred on discipleship, which included chapters or sections on prayer. In retirement I have decided to donate many of these books as a collection to the library of my Seminary. However, as I was looking over the shelves of books, I asked myself two questions – "who are these unknown and lesser known authors and what prompted them to write on prayer?" Then another question – "will this generation and future generations be blessed by what is in these books?" That is when I decided to compile this collection of quotes and comments.

While you may recognize a few names of authors, many will be unknown, and the names you recognize, will be unknown to others. Some will have published works several years before you started reading books on prayer. Actually all of the quotes in this volume are from books published prior to 2005. Also, you may disagree with a few of the authors. It's OK. I disagreed with a few myself. Just read again on the next day, and perhaps you will be in more agreement with the next author.

So, I began the task of searching through these books to see what meaningful comments I or previous owners had underlined or highlighted; checking pages with the top corner turned down. This book then is a collection of those quotes.

I trust you will be challenged by these quotes, strengthened by them, edified by them, and that each quote will provide meaningful ideas that hopefully will enhance your own prayer life.

JANUARY

January 1

"The beginning point of genuine prayer – a desire to reach out to God. The real quest of prayer is to know God, not to get stuff. . . Prayer is interpersonal communication between a person and God. All of the open intimacy implied in communication is present. This includes everything from humor to anger, from request to praise."

> **Don M Aycock**, *Prayer 101*. Nashville: Broadman & Holman Publishers, 1998, p. 22.

January 2

"Seeking and finding may be a risky business for you. It is so much more secure to stay where you are. But, there are things of God we cannot have until we are ready to leave the security of what God has done for the insecurity of what he is doing and will do."

> **Bill Austin**, *How to Get What You Pray For.* Wheaton: Tyndale House Publishers, 1984, p. 161.

January 3

"Prayer is a conversation of the heart with God. Through prayer we align ourselves with our Creator, and His presence is revealed to us. We grow in our love and worship of Him. And when we are united with our Lord through prayer, our life becomes fuller, richer, more joyous and more peaceful."

> **James P. Gillis**, *The Prayerful Spirit*. Tarpon Springs, FL: Love Press, 1994, p. 1.

January 4

"God has feelings, too. He welcomes prayer. But prayer to God is about love and relationship and communication, not about making God into a celestial genie in a prayer bottle who will grant our wishes when we ask. It's true that changes do come from a personal relationship with God and that prayer is an important means to change. But that is secondary to what prayer is essentially about. Prayer would be a glorious and wonderful privilege even if nothing changed, just because prayer is our means of connecting with God. Prayer is primarily about God, not primarily about change."

> **Leith Anderson**, *When God Says No*. Minneapolis: Bethany House Publishers, 1996, p. 155.

January 5

"Prayer . . . must have act and will at the centre of it, must be more than a mere state of mind, if it is to be the relation of a self to God, i.e., a genuine personal relationship. The expression of such selfhood even in the very presence of the Eternal, is petition."

> **Herbert H. Farmer**, *The World and God*. London: Nisbet, 1936, p. 135.

January 6

"Few people seek prayer from the church anymore. Many come for groceries, for clothes, for shelter, for friendship. Few come for prayer. We seem to think we don't need prayer anymore. It has become a ritual or a pastime. But prayer is a weapon, a source of power much stronger than the budgets and programs we put our faith in,"

> **R. Earl Allen**, *Prayers that Changed History*. Nashville: Broadman Press, 1977, p. 47.

January 7

"To many Christians, prayer is a spiritual life preserver. In case of an emergency it's the first thing we reach for. But in our daily circumstances we store that life preserver away."

> **Tom Carter**, *They Knew How to Pray*. Grand Rapids: Baker Book House, 1991, p. 154.

January 8

"Prayer is something more than an exterior act performed out of a sense of duty, an act in which we tell God various things he already knows . . . even though Christians find, to their pain and sorrow, that their prayer never rises above this level, they know well enough that it should be something more."

Hans Urs von Balthasar, *Prayer.* Translated by A.V. Littledale. London: SPCK, 1961, p. 11.

January 9

"Whenever there is an extraordinary movement of God among his people, either to reform them, awaken them, use them for a good harvest of the lost or to accomplish some uncommon good or justice within society, it is as a rule, accompanied by an extraordinary movement of prayer."

Robert Bakke, *The Concert of Prayer: Back to the Future.* Minneapolis: Evangelical Free Church of America, 1993, p. 7.

January 10

"Let me not, when this morning prayer is said, think my worship ended and spend the day in forgetfulness of Thee. Rather from these moments of quietness let light go forth, and joy, and power, that will remain with me though all the hours of the day."

John Baille, *A Diary of Private Prayer.* New York: Charles Scribner's Sons, 1949, p. 9.

January 11

"Fellow-laborers in His vineyard, it is quite evident that our Master desires us to ask, and to ask much. He tells us we glorify God by doing so! Nothing is beyond the scope of prayer which is not beyond the will of God – and we do not desire to go beyond His will."

An Unknown Christian, *The Kneeling Christian.* Grand Rapids: Zondervan Publishing House, n.d., p. 19.

January 12

"Satan has no defense against this secret weapon; he does not have an anti-prayer missile. For instance, the unbeliever has many defenses against our evangelistic efforts. He can refuse to attend church, and if he does occasionally show up, he can shift into neutral and count the cracks on the ceiling. You can go to his home, but he doesn't have to let you in. Hand him a tract on the street, and he can throw it away. Get on TV, and he can switch channels. Call him on the phone, and he can hang up. But he cannot prevent the Lord Jesus from knocking on the door of his heart in response tour intercession."

> **Ron Dunn**, *Don't Just Stand There, Pray Something*. San Bernardino, CA: Here's Life, 1991, p. 20.

January 13

"We don't have to impress God, or use big words, or pray long prayers. We don't have to repeat ourselves when we pray, and we don't have to worry about getting all the details correct or throw in flowery language when we pray. Since God knows us through and through, he knows our needs better than we do. When you pray, you aren't informing God of anything. He knew your need before you bowed your head."

> **Ray Pritchard**, *And When You Pray*. Nashville: Broadman & Holman, 2002, p. 17.

January 14

"For the disciples of Jesus there is the Master . . . who teaches prayer, who stands midway between the prophet and the final eschatological figure. With the former he has in common a life and work among the people of God, like a prophet he preaches the Word of God in his time and associates it with earlier revelations in whose strength he lives and which he makes his own. With the final eschatological figure, on the other hand, he stands aside from tradition and begins something new."

> **Ernst Lohmeyer**, translated by John Bowen, *The Lord's Prayer*. London: Collins, 1952, pp. 23-24.

January 15

"The reward for secret prayer is the prayer itself, the blessing of resting in the presence of God. Prayer does not simply maintain the Christian life, it is the Christian life, reduced to its barest essence. Can there be any greater joy – in this world or the next – than to commune in the secret place with the living God?"

> **Philip Graham Ryken**, *When You Pray*. Wheaton: Crossway Books, 2000, p. 21.

January 16

"Why isn't prayer making a greater difference . . . perhaps it is because so few of us really understand the importance of prayer. We do not see prayer as the key factor in building the church or changing the world. We are so self-confident and 'sufficient in ourselves' that we neglect prayer and attempt to do things for God in our own way and in our own strength. Of course, we'd like for God to bless our efforts, so we add a little prayer, seeking his support. But that isn't God's way. His way involves earnest, constant, devoted, striving, powerful prayer. That's what makes a real difference in the world around us."

> **Alvin J, Vander Griend**, *Make Your Home a Light-House.* Grand Rapids: Houses of Prayer Everywhere, 1999, p. 6.

January 17

"'If' is the weakest word in the world. Does it denote faith, bold positive assurance, dynamic expectancy that must surely thrill the heart of God? Or does it show doubt, hesitation and uncertainly? Many wonderful prayers have gone unanswered because they were rendered powerless with the word 'if' in the middle of them."

> **John R. Bisagno**, *The Power of Positive Praying.* Grand Rapids: Zondervan Publishing House, 1965, p. 20.

January 18

"You do not need to pray to inform God about the need that burdens you, for God knows the whole situation better than you do . . . You need to pray because God has ordained to work through your prayer, added to the intercession of Jesus at the Father's right hand."

> **Wesley L. Duewel**, *Mighty Prevailing Prayer.* Grand Rapids: Francis Asbury Press, 1990, p. 301.

January 19

"It is my contention that you can tell what is really important to someone by listening to what he prays for. We spend so much time praying for safety on the highways, good health for each other, solutions to our problems, for the gift and the giver, but we never get down to real matters of faith . . . Jesus understood that the central core of a person's being is his faith. With faith he can face the worst sifting Satan can dish out. Without it he will be blown away in the first breeze."

> **Paris Donehoo**, *Prayer in the Life of Jesus*. Nashville: Broadman Press, 1984, pp. 54-55.

January 20

"It is essential to make of prayer what it is meant to be: a face to face conversation with God. We should be concerned about attaining this; we should not waver in our firm determination to seek God, and God alone. Neither dryness nor consolations can relieve us of this obligation."

> **A.M. Besnard**, *Take a Chance on God: A Guide to Christian Prayer*. Denville, NJ: Dimension Books, 1977, p. 47.

January 21

"Prayer is our personal response to God's presence. We approach the Lord reverently with a listening heart. God speaks first. In prayer, we acknowledge the Divine presence and in gratitude respond to God in love. The focus is always on God and on what God does."

> **Jacqueline Syrup Bergan**, *Surrender: A Guide for Prayer*. Winona, MN: Saint Mary's Press, 1986, p. 1.

January 22

"So often we look to others, especially to Christian leaders, to hear from God for us, instead of taking time to hear from Him ourselves . . . We must grow more mature in our relationship with God, while at the same time maintaining our childlike quality of faith. One way we can do this is to take time to hear from God ourselves."

> **Rita Bennett**, *Inner Wholeness through the Lord's Prayer*. Terrytown, NY: Fleming H. Revell Company, 1991, p. 176.

January 23

"One fact is certain these days: We could all use divine intervention in our lives. Prayer makes such intervention possible . . . Authentic prayer brings heavenly realities to bear on earthly situations."

> Bob Beltz, *Becoming a Man of Prayer*. Colorado Springs: Navpress, 1996, p. 45.

January 24

"If it is a fact that I must pray, and shall pray when 'cornered' by circumstances, then the better I pray the better for me – let me master the practice while there is leisure and time, remembering that here as elsewhere only practice makes perfect."

> **Albert D. Belden**, *The Practice of Prayer.* New York: Harper & Bros. 1954, p. 14.

January 25

"Nothing would turn the nation back to God so surely and so quickly as a Church that prayed and prevailed. The world will never believe in a religion in which there is no supernatural power. A rationalized faith, a socialized church, and a moralized gospel may gain applause, but they awaken no conviction and win no converts."

> **Samuel Chadwick**, *The Path to Prayer*. Kansas City: Beacon Hill Press, 1931, p. 89.

January 26

"No greater evidence of the mighty transformation that is wrought by salvation can be found than the fact that the privilege is granted to the one who is saved of entering the holist place where Christ is already entered in, and is there making intercession for His own who are in the world. Only those who have partaken of the divine nature by regeneration and have come, by grace, to be heavenly in being and destiny could be so favored."

> **Lewis Sperry Chafer**, *True Evangelism: Winning Souls by Prayer.* Grand Rapids: Kregel Publications, 1993, p. 64.

January 27

"The prayer link between the Body of Christ and the Godhead has grown weaker instead of stronger. Our prayers, too often have degenerated into tedious recitations of 'wish lists' instead of exciting, two-way dialogues and strategic planning sessions with the Creator of the universe."

Brother Andrew, *And God Changed His Mind*. Old Tappan, NJ: Fleming H. Revell Company, 1990, p. 28.

January 28

"Real supplication is the child of heartfelt desire, and cannot prevail without it; a desire not of earth nor issuing from our sinful hearts, but wrought unto us by God himself . . . An earnest desire in spiritual things is a bell ringing for prayer. Not that we should wait for such desires. We should pray at all seasons, whether we are prayer hungry or not. If we have a healthy prayer appetite, so much the better."

> **Mrs. O. J. Fraser**, *Fraser and Prayer*. London: Overseas Missionary Fellowship, 1963, pp.33-34.

January 29

"Many Christians honestly believe that 'Prayer pays,' and that 'Prayer is power,' but eventually become discouraged when it seems they are merely hollering through a pipe with no one listening at the other end. But the moment people hear something from the other end, their interest in prayer is renewed and their faith is strengthened. Prayer truly is a two-way communication, and God wants to speak to His children."

> **Christopher J. Christianson**, *God Did Not Ordain Silence*. Plainfield, NJ, 1974, p. 8.

January 30

"Prayer and the Word of God go hand in hand in the Christian life, as well as in Scripture. This is only reasonable since in prayer we speak to God and in the Bible, he speaks to us. Prayer and Scriptures are the vehicles by which we enjoy communication with God. Prayer is the term that the Bible uses to describe our side of the conversation, and Scripture contains God's most important words to us."

> **Thomas L. Constable**, *Talking to God*. Grand Rapids: Baker Books, 1995, p. 67.

January 31

"We can spend fruitless hours in prayer if our hearts are not prepared beforehand. Preparation of the heart, the spirit, comes from meditation in the Father's Word, meditation on who we are in Christ, what He is to us, and what the Holy Spirit can mean to us as we become God-inside minded."

> **Germaine Copeland**, *Prayers That Avail Much*. Tulsa: Harrison House, Inc., 1989, p. 21.

FEBRUARY

February 1

"Prayer and spiritual life are as inseparable as breath and natural life. Wherever one is there is also the other. Yet the prayer periods of so many of us are separated by such long intervals that we hold onto spiritual life by a scant thread."

> **R. L. Brandt**, *Praying with Paul*. Grand Rapids: Baker Book House, 1966, p. 99.

February 2

"Our praying often suffers from sameness. We pray in the same place, in the same way, at the same times, for the same things, with the same people – sameness. As with most things in life, variety helps."

> **Edward C. Briggs**, *A Pilgrim's Guide to Prayer*. Nashville: Broadman Press, 1987, p. 69.

February 3

"God has wisely and purposefully built a beautiful diversity into the unity of His people and your unique gifting and personality can impact how you pray. Prayer is basically a communication vehicle we use to develop our relationship with God. The way any individual relates best to God through prayer will bear similarities to the way he or she most naturally relates to friends and family."

> **Dee Duke**, *Prayer Quest: Breaking Through to Your God-given Dreams and Destiny*. Colorado Springs: Navpress, 2004, p. 63.

February 4

"One of the most startling truths about prayer is this: prayer can be taught and learnt. Once the disciples have enjoyed the opportunity to observe Jesus at prayer, they ask him to teach them how to pray, as John the Baptist once taught his disciples to pray . . . he provides them with a model prayer, designed less as a piece of ecclesiastical liturgy than as a teaching device to foster their own praying and provide them with a standard."

> **D.A. Carson**, *Teach Us to Pray*. Grand Rapids: Baker Book House, 1990, p. 13.

February 5

"In a certain sense, we don't really pray unless we ask God for what we cannot bring about ourselves. To petition Him for no more than we can expect to do in our own strength is to make prayer a decidedly lukewarm and impotent exercise and to discourage its use altogether."

> **J. Paul Carleton**, *Rejoicing in Prayer*. Shawnee, OK: Oklahoma Baptist University Press, 1949, p. 37.

February 6

"If our leisure thoughts are habitually of God, if our closing thoughts of the day are of him, if the very warp and woof of our being cries after more of God, then it is clear indeed that God is at work in us twenty-four hours a day."

> **Donald E. Demary**, *How Are You Praying*? Grand Rapids: Francis Asbury Press, 1985, p. 43.

February 7

"Whereas ordinary approaches to prayer begin with time apart from life, noisy contemplation starts in the middle of life. In no way does it reject the value of quiet time apart, but its emphasis is upon developing prayer that can flourish throughout our active days. It treasures time apart from ordinary life to gain perspective. It also celebrates the prayer of perspective that can flow from prayer in the midst of life."

> **William R. Callahan**, *Noisy Contemplation: Deep Prayer for Busy People*. Hyattsville, MD: Quixote Center, Inc., 1982, p. 65.

February 8

"The practice of prayer is the work of a lifetime, touching every aspect of our life, from the search for identity to the challenge of vocation to the acceptance of death. It takes us through the heights, the depths, and the desert – to say nothing of the occasional swamp."

Margaret Guenther, *The Practice of Prayer*. Cambridge – Boston: Cowley Publications, 1998, p. 5.

February 9

"The prayer that intelligently seeks the Presence must be preceded and followed by a life that practices the Presence. What one is outside his prayers will determine what one is inside his prayers. To live hour by hour and day by day as if God were not, is to make it difficult, if not impossible, to meet in prayer the God who is."

Albert Edward Day, *Existence Under God*. New York-Nashville: Abingdon Press, 1958, p. 56.

February 10

"The right background for special prayer in an emergency is the steady habit of daily prayer from which our knowledge of God grows. He who knows God in the intimacy gained from daily intercourse will not lack guidance when, in an emergency or faced by a weighty decision, he turns to Him for special direction."

Donald Coggan, *The Prayers of the New Testament*. Washington-Celevland: Corpus Books, 1967, pp. 16-17.

February 11

"Faith in God naturally leads to adoration. Prayer without adoration is like a body without a soul. It is not only incomplete, but it just doesn't work. Through adoration we express our genuine, heartfelt love and longing for God."

Hank Hanegraaff, *The Prayer of Jesus*. Nashville: W Publishing Group, 2001, p. 23.

February 12

"Almost every person has some knowledge about prayer. Many people would like to pray, but they sense that they have no access to God. To the true Christian, however, prayer is life's highest and holiest privilege and greatest delight.

G. Christian Weiss, *Progress in Prayer*. Lincoln, NB: Back to the Bible, 1965, p. 16.

February 13

"Incense can neither smell nor ascend without fire; no more does prayer unless it arises from spiritual warmth and fervency . . . Cold, lifeless, and idle prayers are like birds without wings . . .mere lip prayers are lost prayers."

J.W. Acker, *Teach Us to Pray.* St. Louis: Concordia, 1961, 31, 33.

February 14

"Prayer is the response and vital side of faith. Believers pray; those who pray believe."

Jan Milic Lochman, translated by Geoffrey W. Bromiley, *The Lord's Prayer*. Grand Rapids: William B. Eerdmans Publishing Company, 1990, p. 5.

February 15

"Holy, revered, praised. If we come into the presence of another human being, if we are sitting down, we rise, bow, salute, but when we come into the presence of God we fall on our knees. We express toward human beings our respect and our esteem. We express toward God our adoration. All our prayers should be in the spirit of adoration."

Gardiner M. Day, *The Lord's Prayer.* Greenwich, CT: The Seabury Press, Inc., 1954, pp. 26-27.

February 16

"Prayer should be the source of your strength and guidance. Your influence in the world will be determined by your prayers . . . Do you want to make a real difference in the world? You can only do so through prayer, as it is what makes a difference in lives and in life events."

Jay Dennis with Marilyn Jeffcoat, *The Prayer Experiment.* Grand Rapids: Zondervan Publishing House, 2001, p. 47.

February 17

"We are all prodigal sons until we learn how to pray – far from our true home, separated from our true center, alienated from our true self. Even if we live and move in the general vicinity of God, until we learn to pray we are like tourists or strangers walking about on our Father's premises without knowing whose place it really is, without realizing the true status He has conferred upon us: that of the sons and daughters of the living Lord of creation."

> **Kenneth O. Eaton**, *Men Who Talked With God*. New York – Nashville: Abingdon Press, 1964, p. 7.

February 18

"There is power in praise which prayer does not have. Of course, the distinction between the two is artificial . . . The highest expression of faith is not prayer in its ordinary sense of petition, but prayer it its sublimest expression of praise."

> **F. J. Huegel**, *Successful Praying*. Minneapolis: Bethany House, 1959, pp. 45, 48.

February 19

"It is through the Scriptures and prayer that our fellowship with God is maintained. If we willfully neglect or disobey the word of God, our prayers, which should delight the Lord, will instead be an abomination to Him. We cannot expect that God will answer our prayers if, while we are calling to him, we refuse to listen to him call to us through his word,"

> **Leroy Eims**, *Prayer: More than Just Words*. Colorado Springs: Navpress, 1982, p. 20.

February 20

"Prayer is that instinctive impulse of the human soul that reaches out after God. It expresses itself in different forms and with varying degrees of distinctiveness which are influenced by the background of our own experience."

> **Grover Carlton Emmons**, *Alone with God*. Nashville: The Upper Room, 1945, p. 5.

February 21

"Prayer and power are inseparable. If you want power, you must pray. He who prays will have all the power of the Holy Spirit upon him. We may have all the truths concerning the Gospel, but if the truths are to be real in our lives and to be set on fire to meet the needs of people around us, we must be ignited by the fires of the Holy Spirit through prayer."

Theodore W. Engstrom, *Workable Prayer Meeting Programs*. Grand Rapids: Zondervan Publishing House, 1955, p. 25

February 22

"Prayer begins with God; what God is and does is the controlling factor in prayer. This must be, since prayer is the approach of man to God as he seeks God's fellowship, favor, help, and approval. Intercourse with God can never spring from what man is, desires, hopes, or purposes."

Fred L. Fisher, *Prayer in the New Testament*. Philadelphia: The Westminster Press. 1954, p. 11.

February 23

"Unspecific prayer is usually lifeless prayer. If we don't know where we ae going, we won't recognize when we arrive, so we just aimlessly wander in the prayer circuit, hoping that something good will happen. We have all prayed those dull, nondirective, uninteresting prayers that accomplish nothing. This is not God's will for us. Prayer can be animated and very much alive if we bring Scriptures into our praying."

Judson Cornwall, *Praying the Scriptures*. Orlando: Creation House, 1988, pp. 172-173.

February 24

"A good assembly – like a good jet engine – is meant for great altitude and for a strong, normal cruising speed. Many of our churches have 'engine' problems. They lack power! The prayer life is so low that they do not even have enough prayer-thrust to get airborne!"

Armin R. Gesswein, *With One Accord in One Place*. Harrisburg, PA: Christian Publications, Inc, 1978, p. 52.

February 25

"A prayer warrior can pray for a thing to be done without necessarily being willing for the answer to come through himself; and he is not even bound to continue in the prayer until it is answered. But an intercessor is responsible to gain his objective, and he can never be free till he has gained it. He will go to any lengths for the prayer to be answered."

Norman P. Grubb, *Rees Howells Intercessor*. Fort Washington, PA: Christian Literature Crusade, 1952, p. 103.

February 26

"Exhaustive research by biblical scholars . . . has demonstrated that in all the huge literature of ancient Judaism there is not one instance of God bring addressed as *abba*. He was called . . . many other exalted titles, but a word like *abba* was too personal, too familiar and intimate to be appropriate. The Lord was high and lifted up, the incomparable One. He was to be approached with reverence and awe. To call him 'Daddy' was unthinkable blasphemy. Yet Jesus prayed like this all the time."

W. Bingham Hunter, *The God Who Hears*. Downers Grove: IVP Books, 1986, p. 97.

February 27

"Perhaps the greatest hindrance of all to answered prayer is lack of faith. We just do not believe that God is going to answer prayer. We have our set ways of prayer. We know how to pray, but how much real trust in God is in our praying?"

Ord L. Morrow, *Hindrances to Answered Prayer*. Lincoln, NB: Back to the Bible, 1985, p.53.

February 28

"Don't be deceived by your enemy, the devil, who hates prayer more than anything you do for the Lord because prayer is the means by which you immediately communicate with God, receiving His life as your own and giving His life to others."

Kathleen G. Grant, *Praying in the Word of God*. Englewood, CO: Prayer Partners with God Publishing, 2004, p. 189.

MARCH

March 1

"The idea of intercessory prayers creates problems even for some of the most devout believers. How can God hear each and every prayer that is being offered at one and the same time? Surely some of those prayers and petitions are in many ways contradictory and will only serve to cancel each other out? ... We make bold to intercede for others because of what we fundamentally believe about God as our loving Father, who works directly, but also through men and women, using their co-operation. In the end, intercession depends upon a life of faith, not in words."

> **Donald Gray**, *All Majesty and Power*. Grand Rapids – Cambridge: William B. Eerdmans Company, 2000, p. 18.

March 2

"A prayer is not a request of God to alter his eternal purposes or to form new ones. It is simply the taking on of an attitude of active dependence – stating your need honestly and fervently, asking according to God's will and leaving the rest with him . . . The Lord's will is the central matter in prayer, not your will . . . Yet since he is a gentle and loving Lord, God's desire is to hear your prayers given in a spirit of active dependence."

> **Evan B. Howard**, *Praying the Scriptures*. Downers Grove: InterVarsity Press, 1999, p. 101.

March 3

"When it comes to prayer, feeling is not the most important thing. Feelings are fickle, easily influenced by health, morale, weather and mood. Prayer is too important to be put at the mercy of our feelings . . . The purpose of prayer is to maintain our relationship with God, not merely to express our feelings . . . Its purpose is not to ventilate our feelings but to celebrate our fellowship with God."

> **David Allan Hubbard**, *The Practice of Prayer*. Downers Grove: Intervarsity Press, 1983, p. 63.

March 4

"Prayer is looking at God, who is ever present, and letting Him look on us."

> **Gerhard Tersteegen**, *The Quiet Way*. New York: Philosophical Library, 1950, p. 23.

March 5

"Did you know that the Lord is interested in the smallest, most 'seemingly' insignificant need of our life. So, don't feel guilty going to Him for your so-called small needs. He wants to hear and answer every prayer."

> **Rick Ingle**, *Heavens of Brass: When Our Prayers do not Reach Heaven*. Anderson, SC: Palmetto Publishing Company, 1974, p. 77.

March 6

"Do you realize that God desires all people to be saved? His heart's desire is that none should perish but that all should come to repentance. So why are there not more people being saved now? Much of the fault, I believe, must be placed on those of us who are Christians, because we do not know how to pray effectively either for lost men and women or for weak Christians."

> **Theodore H. Epp**, *Praying with Authority*. Lincoln, NB: Back to the Bible, 1965, p. 59.

March 7

"Prayer is so mysterious to some people they expect deep theological treatises and confusing philosophical constructions in any discussion of it. But the secrets of prayer are not mysterious because they are so complex. They are mysterious because they are so simple."

> **Paris Donehoo**, *Prayer in the Life of Jesus*. Nashville: Broadman Press, 1984, p. 7.

March 8

"Just as the loss of appetite is a danger signal in health, so weak and desultory desire is a danger signal in devotional life. We have all heard petitions which were perfectly proper in the objects sought and in the way they were phrased but woefully pathetic in their lack of fervor."

Ralph A. Herring, *The Cycle of Prayer*. Nashville: Broadman Press, 1966, p. 42.

March 9

"I am quite sure there is value in deliberately bowing the knee and bowing the head. When you are seeking to adore God in your own heart it seems right and fitting that your knee should be bowed and your head bowed with it."

Geoffrey R. King, *Let Us Pray*. Fort Washington, PA: Christian Literature Crusade, n.d., p. 45.

March 10

"Distractions are a real problem in one's quiet time. It is difficult for most folk to hold to one thought for any length of time. We are so far away from formal schooling, the last times that we really practiced concentration that the mind readily wanders. Hence, any little distraction will start the mind wandering . . . Above all, remember that the meditation, even the quiet time, is not an end in itself. It is a time of silence to bring us into the presence of God."

Harold Wiley Freer and Francis B. Hall, *Two or Three Together*. New York, Evanston and London: Harper & Row Publishers, 1954, pp. 113-114.

March 11

"It is safe to say that some of our prayer assignments are also being borne by other Christians. Let's guard our hearts against feeling that we – and our prayers – are 'the only reasons' something happens."

Eddie & Alice Smith, *The Advocates: How to Plead the Case of Others in Prayer*. Lake Mary, FL: Charisma House, 2001, p. 107.

March 12

"Prayer is one of the most important aspects of building disciples. If one is to help men grow in the knowledge of Jesus Christ, he must pray. Indeed, if he does everything else right in terms of building disciples, yet fails to pray, nothing significant will happen. The reason is simple. God acts in response to believing prayer."

Carl Wilson, *With Christ in the School of Disciple Building*. Grand Rapids: Zondervan Publishing House, 1976, p. 223.

March 13

"God feels our sorrows, our misery, our anxiety. He weeps with us. He also feels our elation, our joy, our relief – and He laughs with us. The greatest thing Jesus taught us about God is that He is a God who cares."

Jamie Buckingham, *Miracle Power*. Ann Arbor, MI: Servant Publications, 1988, p. 206.

March 14

"In its earliest incarnations prayer was a way of life that occupied every hour of the day, not simply kneeling in prayer, but as a fabric of life, in thought, in deed, and in relationship with the world."

Philip Dunn, *Prayer: Language of the Soul*. New York: Daybreak Books, 1997, p. 2.

March 15

"The one quality Christian prayer in faith demands from us is not moral excellence nor a spiritual gift nor natural piety but humility, humility to acknowledge our unworthiness of God and our need."

Daniel T. Jenkins, *Prayer and the Service of God*. London: Morehouse-Gorham, 1945, pp. 51-52.

March 16

"If you will ask yourself the question, When do I pray the longer prayers, in public or in secret? The answer may give you some idea as to whether you pray to God or that men may hear."

C.J. Kinne, *Prayer: The Secret of Power*. Kansas City: Nazarene Publishing House, 1913, p. 16

March 17

"Faith is to believe that He cares and He can and does intervene at unexpected places in unexpected ways, but it is not for us to define those places and ways. Only God can decide those things."

Hubert Beck, *What Should I Believe?* St. Louis: Concordia Publishing House, 1980, p. 41.

March 18

"One of the biggest problems many of us face in praising the Lord openly is that of overcoming our natural inhibitions. We almost feel embarrassed to praise God, simply because nobody else is doing it! And all of us understand how difficult it is to do a thing that no one else is doing – especially if it is quite certain that the doing of that thing will bring ridicule from others."

Don Gossett, *There's Dynamite in Praise.* Springdale, PA: Whitaker House, 1974, p. 39.

March 19

"Prayer involves submission to God's will. God's sovereignty clarifies some aspects of prayer for us. God is our king. We are not His electorate. He's not a president, responsible to us for His actions. We are His subjects. We don't advise the king; we obey Him. We should never enter into prayer with the attitude or notion that we are in any way advising or counseling God."

Dandi Daley Knorr, *When the Answer is No.* Nashville: Broadman, 1985, p. 49.

March 20

"Some rather contemptuously contrast the 'pray-ers' with the 'doers,' but they forget that in the history of the Church it has always been the 'pray-ers' who have been the effective 'doers.' The early Church was so dynamic because it was continually in the place of prayer.

D. Edmond Hiebert, *Working with God through Intercessory Prayer.* Greenville, SC: Bob Jones University Press, 1991, p.52.

March 21

"Prayer is something deeper than words. It is present in the soul before it has been formulated in words. And it abides in the soul after the last words of prayer have passed over the lips."

Ole Christian Hallesby, *Prayer.* Translated by Clarence J. Carlsen. Minnesota: Augsburg Publishing House, 1975, p.16.

March 22

"All of your life, whenever there is unusual pressure on you or you are facing some crisis or calamity, the phrases you have thus memorized and used as prayers will rise automatically into your consciousness and become holy food, nourishing your heart."

John Killinger, *Prayer: The Act of Being with God*. Waco, TX: Word Books, 1981, p. 37.

March 23

"The most vital prayer is the one which springs unprompted from the heart; it has no difficulty in finding its own appropriate language. Indeed, we may say that the spontaneous expression of repentance or yearning, adoration or joy, supplication or thanksgiving, is the prime language of prayer."

Romano Guardivi, *Prayer in Practice*. Image Books Edition, 1963, p. 88.

March 24

"Prayer is not the latest fad, the current church-growth technique, or the last-ditch effort to combat an increasingly secular society. Prayer is the expression of our hunger for divine companionship, of our desire for intimacy with our Creator, of our need to build a deeper relationship with our Lord. Prayer is seeking God: surrendering ourselves to God's will, receiving God's gifts and blessings, welcoming God's presence in our lives, expressing our gratitude to God, and interceding on behalf of others in need."

Douglas A. Kamstra, *The Praying Church Idea Book*. Grand Rapids: Faith Alive Christian Resources, 2001, p. 14.

March 25

"Prayer is the way in which we expose our ignorance or our wisdom, our wrong or our right attitudes to God. True prayer always expresses reverence to God, a real sense of need, the suppression of pride and the confidence of being heard by God."

James Houston, *Prayer: The Transforming Friendship*. Oxford, England: Lion Publishing, 1989, p. 259.

March 26

"The strange and beautiful thing about this praying without ceasing is that it goes on all the time as a sort of background for the other business and pleasures of life. It is like some great musical masterpiece being performed upon the piano in which the right hand is engaged in all sorts of runs and thrills while the left hand carries the theme in the steady beat of magnificent chords."

> **Constance Garrett**, *Growth in Prayer*. New York: The Macmillan Company, 1949, p. 99.

March 27

"We don't have to wait until our trials are over to acknowledge God. While we may not be able to erect a monument to point to what God has done and is doing, we are able to offer him a high-five in our hearts and in our praise.:

> **Jay Dennis with Marilyn Jeffcoat**, *The Prayer Experiment*. Grand Rapids: Zondervan Publishing House, 2001, p. 87.

March 28

"Prayer and faith are bound together. They develop through use, not mere discussions. The best preparation for prayer is praying and praying leads us into deeper faith."

> **Nolan R. Howington**, *The Vigil of Prayer*. Nashville: Broadman Press, 1987, p. 57.

March 29

"Prayer is the supreme act of hope. If we pray, we must believe someone is there to hear our prayer and is powerful enough to answer us. Prayer that is permeated with hope hears the inaudible, believes the inconceivable, and expresses the inexpressible. It lifts us from the ditch of despair and transports us to the throne room of God. But prayer without hope is like a sail without wind. It's going nowhere."

> **Woodrow Kroll**, *When God Doesn't Answer*. Grand Rapids: Baker Books, 1997, p. 151.

March 30

"Many of us do a remarkable job of avoiding sin and of following faithfully a spiritual regimen, but year after year we seem to remain in the same spiritual path, if we don't slip backwards! We settle for perseverance when we should be climbing the heights. We get stuck somewhere on the face of the mountain."

> **Charles J. Keating**, *Who we are is How we Pray*. Mystic, CT: Twenty-Third Publications, 1987, p. 1.

March 31

"I believe our emotions – all of them – belong in our prayers . . . Our prayers represent not just what we say but who we are, with all our complex longings and feelings. To be close to someone, even when that someone is God, will inevitably run us through a gamut of emotions. To think prayer should be a monochrome patter is to rob it of its power . . . A wide and sometimes wild range of feelings accompanies a walk with God."

> **Timothy Jones**, *The Art of Prayer*. New York: Ballantine Books, 1997, pp. 122-123.

APRIL

April 1

"Most of us pray when all else fails. We need to have a regular, earnest and persistent prayer life. Our prayer should be more than a few words each day. It should be embodied within us, changing us."

> **James P. Gills**, M.D., *The Prayerful Spirit.* Tarpon Springs, FL: Love Press, 1994, p. 77.

April 2

"For many people, prayer is a consumer commodity. We pray for things: rain, peace, health, success. And when we get what we asked for, we believe our prayer is responsible for it. If we don't get it, we switch to another way of thinking and wonder whether we prayed wrong, or whether God just knew better, or whether someone else deserved to win this one more than we did. We think prayer is something we do to get something else. It's a commodity to be traded for favors from God, who, in our judgement, would not bestow these favors without sufficient supplication."

> **Bill Huebsch**, *A New Look at Prayer.* Mystic, CT: Twenty-Third Publications, 1991, p. 2.

April 3

"Prevailing prayer is not to be confounded with the fretful teasing of a restless heart, unhappy and dissatisfied, crying out rebelliously for changed circumstances that its own comfort may be increased. It is rather the trusting petition of a soul at perfect peace, resting in the very centre of the will of God, asking in happy confidence for what the blessed Holy Spirit knows will bring added glory to God."

> **H.A. Ironside**, *Praying in the Holy Spirit.* New York: Loizeaux Brothers, Publishers, n.d., p. 47.

April 4

"Prayerlessness short-circuits the working of God. In His love, He imposes Himself on no one. He waits to be asked. Neglecting prayer, therefore, is not a weakness; it is a sinful choice. Thank God that the atoning blood of Christ Jesus can remove the guilt of the sin of prayerlessness."

> **Ben Jennings**, *The Arena of Prayer.* Orlando: NewLife Publications, 1999, p.5.

April 5

"Prayer gives you the ability to stand alone with God. You can be physically alone anywhere in the whole world yet, through prayer, immediately discover that you are no longer alone. God, through his Son, Jesus Christ, is right there with you."

> **Francis E. Gardner**, *Hot Line to Heaven.* Anderson, IN: The Warner Press, 1970, p. 97.

April 6

"We can talk more easily to a person that we have come to know and respect and love than we can with the stranger who is distant or of whom we are uncertain."

> **Erwin J. Kolb**, *A Prayer Primer.* St. Louis: Concordia House, 1982, p. 15.

April 7

"You know that's the *danger of prayer*. We pray to God with the confidence that he has the power to answer our prayers. Yet we do not concede him the authority to answer in his own fashion."

> **Ben Haden**, *Pray! Don't Settle for a Two-Bit Prayer Life.* Nashville – New York: Thomas Nelson, Inc., 1974, book has no page numbers.

April 8

"Most of us pray for answers. We face some decision or crisis in life, the way ahead unclear. We long for guidance and pray for an answer. 'God answers prayers,' is the byword and assurance that guides our approach to the throne in prayer, and we bring our intercessions before the One who hears us even before we speak or think.

> **John Indermark**, *Traveling the Prayer Paths of Jesus*. Nashville: Upper Room Books, 2003, p.36.

April 9

"Prayer has two sides, not one as we often suppose. The side which we focus on is *telling*. Certainly telling is an element. Sometimes, perhaps precisely because we learn how to pray from public worship, it is seen as the only element. The other side of prayer, which we often neglect, is *listening*."

> **E. Glenn Hinson**, *The Reaffirmation of Prayer*. Nashville: Broadman Press, 1979, p. 30.

April 10

"In moments of prayer we have direct experiences of the meaning and glory of life. For there we know that God is with us, that He cares, and that what we think and do really matters. In prayer, then, the whole sweep of revealed religion becomes an experienced reality."

> **Mack B. Stokes**, *Talking with God*. Nashville: Abingdon Press, 1989, p. 101

April 11

"As long as I think of prayer as giving orders to God, prayer is an unbearable burden: It puts me in charge of the universe, or at least of my own world. Prayer becomes a relaxed visit with God when I understand that prayer is merely giving God permission to do what He has declared He wants to do. The better I understand His will, the easier it is to pray that will and to submit to it."

> **Judson Cornwall**, *Praying the Scriptures*. Orlando: Creation House, 1988. p. 90.

April 12

"Did you realize that one major way God measures your life is by your intercession? Your earnest prayer can expand your life beyond any other limits that you can reach."

Wesley L. Duewel, *Measure Your Life*. Grand Rapids: Zondervan
Publishing House, 1992, p. 63.

April 13

"Prayer . . . which restores my energies, takes away my fatigue, and which to
the very end makes tranquilizers useless, for it eases every tension, every
conflict."

Jacques Ellul, translated by C. Edward Hopkin, *Prayer and Modern
Man*. New York: Seabury Press, 1970, p. 69.

April 14

"Satan hates prayer and desperately tempts us with the lie that token prayer is
enough . . . Prayer pushes back the kingdom of darkness, protects the people
we pray for, limits Satan's work. The enemy knows that and frantically tries
to convince us that prayer doesn't work, harassing and haranguing in hopes
that we will wear down and give up."

Dee Duke with Brian Smith, *Prayer Quest*. Colorado Springs:
Navpress, 2004, p. 55.

April 15

"There are no 'toy prayers.' Every prayer is genuine, and every prayer
receives the attention of our heavenly Father."

Steve Harper, *Praying through the Lord's Prayer*. Nashville: Upper
Room Books, 1992, p. 17.

April 16

"Prayer is therefore not omnipotent in the sense that, whatever it earnestly
asks, it can secure. It must sincerely subordinate itself to the will of God; and
then whatever the issue, it must remain content, believing that the will is
done."

John Edward McFadyen, *The Prayers of the Bible*. New York: A.C.
Armstrong and Son, n.d., p. 187.

April 17

"There is not a half-formed aspiration or a heavenward impulse that was not first 'inspoken' into the heart by the Spirit who maketh intercession for us. We could not pray aright unless the Lord of Prayer taught us, and the only prayers that remain unanswered are the prayers which He does not inspire."

> **E. Herman**, *Creative Prayer*. New York – Evanston – London: Harper & Row Publishers, n,d., p. 38.

April 18

"Believing we are accepted by God without conditions opens the door to our risking to pray to God in complete honesty. As long as we believe in a God before whom we must constantly 'measure up,' we will never feel the inward freedom to pray openly and honestly."

> **Jan G. Lin**, *Living Inside Out: Learning How to Pray the Serenity Prayer*. St. Louis: Chalice Press, 1994, p. 19

April 19

"Prayer is not just about feeling closer to God and feeling better about the world. It's about allowing God to transform us into the people he has created us to be. For most of us, that means learning to respect and love people who are starkly different than us."

> **Mark Grilli and James S. Bell, Jr.**, *The Complete Idiot's Guide to Prayer*. Indianapolis: Alpha Books, 1999, p. 69.

April 20

"Faith believes not only that God is *able* to do what one petitions him to do, but that God is also *willing* to do it. It is the combination of these two that constitutes faith in its generic and biblical sense. One without the other will hardly do. They must exist together."

> **Harold Lindsell**, *When You Pray*. Wheaton: Tyndale House Publishers, 1969, p. 69.

April 21

"In personal prayer the individual faces God. God has created him and called him into a special relationship in grace with Him. It is by virtue of this relationship, in which God meets each one of us directly, that we rise to the dignity of being individuals at all – of being individual selves. It finds its expression in personal prayer, which is a dialogue between the one individual and God."

> **Romano Guardini**, *Prayer in Practice*. Garden City, NY: Image Books, 1963, p. 149.

April 22

"There is no place where we can love our friends more than at the throne of grace. No other exercise so fully melts away the differences of Christians and brings their hearts together in unity as prayer. There is no remedy for the divisions of Christianity but to come closer to the Father, and then we shall be in touch with each other."

> **A.B. Simpson**, *The Life of Prayer*. Camp Hill, PA: Christian Publications, 1989, p. 14

April 23

"What Satan fears more than anything is prayer. He knows that prayer unleashes the power of God. Because Jesus overcame Satan once and for all on the cross, you and I can exercise our dearly bought right of access in prayer to the Father."

> **Carey Moore and Pamela Rosewell Moore**, *What Happens When Husbands and Wives Pray Together?* Grand Rapids: Fleming H. Revell, 1992, p. 94

April 24

"God is very happy when we pray. The Bible makes it clear that God is glad to hear from us and rejoices over us. He loves us and is delighted when we come before him, just as a loving father is happy when his children come to him. The father welcomes his children with open arms and listens carefully to everything they say because he loves them so much."

> **Daryl Lucas**, General Editor, *107 Questions Children Ask About Prayer*. Wheaton: Tyndale House Publishers, 1998, p. 14.

April 25

"The way to get a thing which is sold is to pay for it; the way to get a thing which is earned is to work for it; the way to get a thing which is given is to ask for it. We live in an age of grace. God's method of blessing His children is not to sell but to give. God's plan for them to receive, is not to buy or even earn, but only to *ask*."

James H. McConkey, *Prayer*. Pittsburgh: Silver Publishing House, 1924, p. 49.

April 26

"We are always in the presence of God. If we live each moment conscious of His presence, we shall not have to readjust our mental attitude when we begin to pray, but we shall pray to the One we have been silently including in our every thought and conversation."

Dorothy C. Haskin, *A Practical Primer on Prayer*, Chicago: Moody Press, 1951, pp. 14-15.

April 27

"Why are there thousands of churches in our country without pastors today? Why are millions in the foreign field yet waiting for the human voice to proclaim to them the everlasting Gospel of the Son of God . . . Why is it so? Because prayer closets are deserted, family altars are broken down, and pulpit prayers are formal and dead!"

Francis McGaw, *Praying Hyde*. Minneapolis: Dimension Fellowship, Inc., 1970, p. 15.

April 28

"When we realize that prayer provides an occasion for God to speak to us, we cannot but ponder the thought that our own Christian service might be more effective if we prayer more often."

Charles M. Laymon, *Great Prayers of the Bible*. Cincinnati: Women's Division of Christian Service, Board of Missions and Church Extension, The Methodist Church, n.d., p. 106.

April 29

"While we are waiting for God to answer, let's ask Him to help us wait with a spirit of expectancy, almost as though we were standing on tiptoe to see what He is going to do. Let's remember that we believe in a supernatural God who loves to do miracles. It is this believing faith that allows us to wait expectantly and creatively until the answer comes – always confident that it *will* come."

> **Hope MacDonald**, *Discovering How to Pray*.   Grand Rapids: Zondervan Publishing House, 1976, pp. 86-87.

April 30

"It **may** well be, that for one reason or another, you will not meet God every morning . . . Please, neither worry nor go out empty-handed into the day. Take one sentence, one phrase, and hold on to it. Say it as often as you can remember it; you may find that something has been given you in the midst of the day which was not found in quiet. After all, God is out there just as surely as he is in the quiet place though we can't always hear him for the noise."

> **H. A. Hamilton**, *Conversation with God*.   New York – Nashville: Abingdon Press, n.d, p. 7.

MAY

May 1

"It's not as of you are telling God anything he does not already know when you admit to him your sins. But it does show that you are sorry for them and that you really do want his forgiveness and are determined (with his help) not to keep on repeating the same old sins, day after day. This time of owning up to your sin is a time to be honest and humble."

> **Mark Water**, *Prayer Made Easy*. Peabody, MA: Hendrickson Publishers, Inc., 1999, p. 12.

May 2

"As you develop in prayer, you will see growth. This will come as you begin to reach out beyond yourself and your family and broaden your self-centered praying to include a wider scope of requests . . . You will start claiming appropriate Scriptures for a situation."

> **Glen Martin & Dian Ginter**, *Power House: A Step-By-Step Guide to Building a Church that Prays*. Nashville: Broadman & Holman Publishers, 1994, p. 99.

May 3

"Unless we can find some place where God is not, and where the telegraph between heaven and earth are beyond reach, there is no place where we should not pray. And unless we can find a place where we do not want God, nor need Him, there is no place where we should not pray."

> **Alexander McLaren**, *Expositions of Holy Scripture*. Grand Rapids: Baker Book House, 1975, vol. 15, p. 354.

May 4

"In our prayers for the sick, not all get well. The danger is that we think that either God did not hear us or that we didn't pray hard enough. The ministry of praying for others is often judged by our successes or failures. That's to play God. Or we stop praying for others because we didn't get what we thought was best when we thought it should happen. Our task is to be faithful and leave the results to God. His timing is perfect and His answers often come in ways we did not expect."

> **Lloyd John Ogilvie**, *Praying with Power*. Ventura, CA: Regal Books, 1983, pp. 100-101.

May 5

"The Christian who meditates on the text of Scripture does not come to it because he does not want God to speak, but because he believes God has already spoken. We enter the presence of God to worship on the basis of a completed revelation, not to acquire more of it. Meditation is not seeking after *revelation*, but *illumination*. The difference is critical."

> **Doug McIntosh**, *God up Close: How to Meditate on His Word*. Chicago: Moody Press, 1998, p. 8.

May 6

"Teaching our children to pray is the first and primary prerequisite to everything else we, as parents, need to teach them. A coach, no matter how good, will never help your children if you don't take them to practice. God is our children's coach, but He can't help them much if we don't take them to prayer."

> **Rick Osborne**, *Teaching Your Children How to Pray*. Chicago: Moody Press 1997, p. 53.

May 7

I've accepted the reality that I'll never learn the perfect method for praying the perfect prayer – the one where I know I'm in the presence of God, I know the Spirit is hearing me, and I can sense that the answers have already begun to swoop toward earth. But I believe in prayer, and it has remained a significant discipline of my life."

> **Cecil Murphey**, *Invading the Privacy of God*. Ann Arbor, MI: Servant Publications, 1997, p. 12.

May 8

"Over the last several years, interest in prayer and spiritual warfare has exploded. Across North America and indeed throughout the world, hundreds of local churches, mission agencies and prayer fellowships have discovered afresh the awesome power of focused intercession . . . It is time to repair the broken altars of your community so the fire of heaven can come down. It is time to prepare for a visitation of the Holy Spirit."

> **George Otis, Jr.**, *Informed Intercession.* Ventura, CA: Renew Books, 1999, pp. 13-14.

May 9

"In ordinary prayer, we ask for the answer to specific needs. We learn to use faith to believe in the healing of causes and painful effects – and often find a Divine response which seems like a miracle. And then, excited by these results, go on into the ever-wider practice of praying about every other trouble as it comes into our orbit . . . Instead of trying to direct His Power into specific pains and problems, we learn to abide in the midst of His Perfection."

> **Brother Mandus**, *The Grain of Mustard Seed.* London: L.N. Fowler & Co. LTD. 1959, p. 101.

May 10

"An answer to prayer becomes a 'miracle' in our eyes when His work breaks out in such obvious fashion that we would have to be afflicted with acute spiritual myopia not to see and acknowledge it . . . But He is working in *all* things."

> **Arnold Prater**, *Learning to Pray.* Nashville: Abingdon Press, 1877, p. 75.

May 11

"Most people when they pray do something which they would consider exceedingly rude in conversation. The go away as soon as they have said their own say and it is the other's turn to speak."

> **Friedrich Rittelmeyer**, translated by S.M.K. Gandell, *The Lord's Prayer.* New York: The Macmillan Company, 1931, p. 24.

May 12

"The greatest challenge facing the church of Jesus Christ today, and therefore every local congregation of believers, is not produced by the great issues of the day. This challenge is not motivating Christians to speak out on contemporary social issues or to become involved in political action, even though such involvement is crucial. Neither is this challenge one of bringing believers into the task of evangelizing the world, even though this task ought to be the concern of all believers. Rather, the greatest challenge facing the church of Jesus Christ today is motivating the people of God to pray."

> **Stanley J. Grenz**, *Prayer: The Cry for the Kingdom*. Peabody, MA: Hendrickson Publishers, 1988, p. 1.

May 13

"There is awesome power in prayer. Through prayer, God's power is released to work mightily within and through us, bringing us to the fullness of our potential in Christ and releasing us to accomplish God's purposes in this world. When we pray, we are on holy ground."

> **Kirkie Morrissey**, *On Holy Ground*. Colorado Springs: Navpress, 1983, p. 21.

May 14

"When we are trying to touch the all-powerful, all-energized hem of God's garment in prayer, force will not help much. It may even cause a spiritual short-circuit. We often try to force God to do things for us because many of us never pray until we are deep in trouble. When we are in that condition our nerves are unstrung, our patience is gone, our thinking us unreliable, so we bang impatiently on God's door."

> **Austin Pardue**, *Prayer Works*. New York: Morehouse-Gorham Co., 1949, pp. 14-15.

May 15

"The answers to the prayers you pray today will be answered in the lives of your descendants at the right time. Those answers will be working in their lives as if you had just prayed them. Your prayers will put spiritual riches on deposit for them."

Jennifer Kennedy Dean, *Legacy of Prayer.* Birmingham: New Hope Publishers, 2002, pp. 29-30.

May 16

"Our Lord takes it for granted that His people will pray. And indeed in Scripture generally the outward obligation of prayer is implied rather than asserted. Moved by divinely-implanted instinct, out natures cry out for God, for the living God. And however this instinct may be crushed by sin, it awakes to power in the consciousness of redemption."

D.M. M'Intyre, *The Hidden Life of Prayer.* Minneapolis: Bethany Fellowship, Inc.,n.d., p. 20.

May 17

"All of us who over the years have prayed have our assurances concerning answered prayer. Sometimes we have asked amiss. Sometimes our heart has not been in the prayer we have prayed with our lips. Sometimes we have asked in unbelief, doubting. Sometimes we have sought our own will, and not the will of God. Yet an answer has come. Sometimes it has been a plain 'No' . . . Sometimes it has been 'Wait.'"

Cyril H. Powell, *Secrets to Answered Prayer.* New York: Thomas T. Crowell Company, 1958, p. 11.

May 18

"Prayer is a mighty enabler of God; and, one of prayer's greatest ministries is the way it allows God to be our Father and allows us to be His child."

Eddie Deitz, *What Does Prayer Enable God to Do?* Cherokee, NC: Mountain Gospel Publishing, 1997, p. 105.

May 19

"The prayers of the apostles are short ones. Not some, or even most, but all of them are exceedingly brief, most of them encompassed in but one or two verses, and the longest in only seven verses. How this rebukes the lengthy, lifeless and wearisome prayers of many a pulpit. Words prayers are usually windy ones."

A.W. Pink, *Effectual Fervent Prayer*. Grand Rapids: Baker Book House, 1981, p. 18.

May 20

"Do you sometimes feel that prayer has nothing to do with real life? After all, we live in a modern world that has little patience with people who pray. At times the world's cynicism leads us to doubt that communication with God has any bearing on our lives . . . The Bible teaches that prayer is immensely relevant. It is not time wasted but a crucial ingredient in our walk with Christ."

Richard L. Pratt, Jr., *Pray with Your Eyes Open*. Phillipsburg, NJ: Presbyterian and Reformed Publishing Company, 1987, p. 67.

May 21

"In everyday life there are times of joy when words are not enough and when feelings are better expressed with a smile or a hop or a hug or some joyful sound. Prayer is sometimes the same; all you can do is exist, breathe, and praise. At other times you may be anxious for someone but have no words to express it. Never mind. Hold that person up and look at God without trying to say anything."

Linette Martin, *Practical Praying*. Grand Rapids: William B. Eerdmans Publishing Company, 1997, p. 89.

May 22

"Most writings on prayer make the experience sound too easy. Those who use it as a spare tire, only when emergencies arise, are disappointed in its results. Prayer is a difficult skill. No complicated skill is mastered by hit or miss methods. Prayer must be made a regular and regulative part of life."

William R. Parker, *Prayer Therapy*. Redlands, CA: W.R. Parker, 1953, p. 45.

May 23

"If it were not for the church, Satan would already have turned this earth into hell. That at least a remnant of the Church is effectively functioning and already has entered upon her rulership in union with her Lord. She is even now, by virtue of the scheme of prayer and faith, engaged in 'on-the-job' training for her place as co-sovereign with Christ over the entire universe following Satan's final destruction."

> **Paul E. Bellheimer**, *Destined for the Throne*. Fort Washington, PA: Christian Literature Crusade, 1975, p. 62.

May 24

"The joy of experiencing God in prayer is not an end in itself but is the water by which the virtues are strengthened and brought to full flowering."

> **Thomas H. Green**, *When the Well Runs Dry.* Notre Dame: Ave Maria Press, 1979, p. 67

May 25

"We are in a fierce conflict with the powers of darkness for the control of human minds. And I have found by experience that God's Holy Spirit alone can bring victory here. Through intercessory prayer I have seen the way open for God to exercise His divine grace toward most underserving individuals."

> **Roger J. Morneau**, *The Incredible Power of Prayer*. Hagerstown, MD: Review and Herald Publishing Association, 1997, p. 63.

May 26

"Prayer is the way God gives us his choicest blessings. It is a way whereby his work grows and prospers. Our lives are meager and bare spiritually, simply because we do not pray."

> **E.W. Price, Jr.**, *ACTS in Prayer*. Nashville: Broadman Press, 1974, p. 6.

May 27

"It is an over-simplification to describe prayer as 'talking to God.' Yet just as a child needs time to learn how to talk, so the art of prayer is something which can take many years to learn. That is why the disciples asked Jesus, 'Lord, teach us to pray.'"

> **Michael Counsell**, Editor, *2000 Years of Prayer*. Harrisburg, PA: Morehouse Publishing, 1999, p. xxvi.

May 28

"God is able to do exceedingly abundantly more than we can ask or think. It is nothing less than an insult to His omnipotence when our prayers are for pitifully little things. We should ask for big things . . . immense things . . . far reaching things. Of course, these things must be in His will, for His glory."

> **William W. Orr**, *How to Pray and Get the Answer.* Wheaton: Scripture Press Publications, Inc., n.d., p. 32.

May 29

"The biblical words for prayer are notable for the way in which they picture the relationship between God and those who trust in Him. God is all-powerful, able to act on man's behalf. God is caring, deeply concerned for our welfare. This God can and will answer the prayers addressed to Him."

> **Larry Richards**, *Every Prayer and Petition in the Bible.* Nashville: Thomas Nelson Publishers, 1998, p. 16.

May 30

"If we knew how to listen to God, if we knew how to look around us, our whole life would become prayer. For it unfolds under God's eyes and no part of it must be lived without being freely offered to him."

Michael Quoist, translated by Agnes M. Forsyth and Anne Marie de Commaille, *Prayers.* New York: Sheed and Ward, Inc., 1963, p.29.

May 31

"If God is omnipotent, can't He send missionaries forth without out prayers? The question evades the issue. God, in His omniscience, has willed that men and woman co-operate with Him in both proclaiming and praying. Jesus commanded us to pray that God would send forth laborers into His harvest, because such prayer is essential in the plan which God has ordained for the reaching of the unreached and the winning of the lost to Christ. God puts Himself at our disposal and does not do His work apart from our prayers."

> **Wentworth Pike**, *Principles of Effective Prayer.* Fort Washington. PA: Christian Literature Crusade, 1983, p. 69.

JUNE

June 1

"Prayer means developing an attitude of gratitude. People who are sour on life have never learned to be grateful, and so they see only the darkest side of life. If you have a heart filled with fear, then you will see a world characterized by fear. If you have a heart filled with love, then you will perceive the world as a loving, secure place in which to dwell. It's up to you how you view life, just as it is up to you to learn how to integrate this sacred element of prayer into your life and make it part of your daily rituals."

Ron Roth, *Prayer and the Five Stages of Healing*. Carlsbad, CA – Sydney, Australia: Hay House, Inc., 1999, p. 180.

June 2

"I wonder if we would be happy if our prayers were published so that others could read them . . . What if all of the prayers that you ever prayed, word for word, were accessible so that anyone, anywhere could read them? Would our prayers be worth reading if they were posted in the Internet? And would they be like those found in the pages of Holy Scripture, or would they more likely fit the *National Enquirer?*"

Ray Pritchard, *Beyond All You Could Ask or Think*. Chicago: Moody Publishers, 2004, p. 71.

June 3

"Our prayers are utterly essential for the outworking of God's good purpose on earth. He is, of course, all powerful, but he has limited himself to work in partnership with human beings to whom he has given the over-sight of the earth. Scripture makes it clear that we are in a dynamic, ongoing relationship with God, not subject to blind faith, fatalistically accepting whatever comes. Through the exercise of the authority Jesus gives us in prayer, we can change our world and its future."

John D. Robb & James A. Hill, *The Peacemaking Power of Prayer*. Nashville: Broadman & Holman, 2000, p. 8.

June 4

"Like some mighty motive power that lies neglected, waiting to be attached to the vast machinery of manufacture, Prayer in Jesus' Name is the unused force for the individual and church life, the motor equal to all the demands of our spiritual machinery."

>**Arthur T. Pierson**, *Lessons in the School of Prayer.* St. Louis: Miracle Press, 1971, p. 83.

June 5

"The Lord Jesus Christ in prayer! What a wonderful theme for study and contemplation! Prayer was the messenger He was wont to send on all His errands, and in this He is an example to us. By prayer He held His constant intercourse with heaven; and we have no better way of doing so. Prayer was the arrow of Christ's deliverance, and the shield of His help. – 'Lord, teach us how to pray.'"

>**Marcus Rainsford**, *Our Lord Prays for His Own.* Chicago: Moody Press, 1950, p. 35.

June 6

"We never need to inform God of the facts that He knows in toto, far beyond any knowledge we may have of even our personal lives. But it is a relief and a great comfort to talk things over with such a God, as our Father in heaven has revealed Himself to be through Jesus Christ."

>**Mrs. S. H. Askew**, *Great Bible Prayers.* Atlanta: Board of Woman's Work, Presbyterian Church in the United States, n.d., p. 30.

June 7

"Prayer is the means by which the gap between God and the human world is overcome. If we do not pray, this widens into an abyss . . . to pray means to overcome distance . . . to heal the break between God and the world."

>**Terry LeFevre**, *Understandings of Prayer. Philadelphia: Westminster Press,* 1981, p. 173.

June 8

"In the book of Acts, the early church was awakened, equipped, and mobilized to pray. They prayed in the temple, in one another's homes, and in the streets. They even had a special room where they assembled for prayer . . . The Upper Room was filled with activity; people were always coming and going . . . The Upper Room became a launching pad for the church's mission."

> **Cheryl Sacks**, *The Prayer Saturated Church*. Colorado Springs: Navpress, 2002, p. 16.

June 9

"As there is no special form of prayer, so also there are no special chosen people whom God hears, nor are there any special places which God has chosen that prayers offered there would be answered. God does not look at the place from whence the prayer goes up, but He looks into the heart that prays, and at the needs of the praying one."

> **N. I. Saloff-Astakhoff**, *The Secret and Power of Prayer*. Chicago: Good News Publishers, 1948, p. 61.

June 10

"So often people try to 'capture' God. For example, if people have experienced a deep conversion as a particular place or when praying a particular way, they often will go back to that same place or repeat their actions, believing that God will again grace them. However, what they have not yet learned is that they are interacting with a personal God who sheds his grace where and when he wills. Going back to a special place to have another spiritual experience is missing the point altogether."

> **Stephen J. Rossetti**, *I am Awake: Discovering Prayer*. New York: Paulist Press, 1987, p. 73.

June 11

"There seems to be a tendency for many Christians to imagine that a church can be conducted and led in the same way as a business concern . . . but the Church of Jesus Christ can only be led in blessing and power by men who have been humbled and broken at the cross, and who, through many experiences of their own failure and nothingness, have learned an utter dependence upon God, and have been taught by the Holy Spirit to lay hold of Him at the Throne of Grace."

> **Alan Redpath**, *Victorious Praying*. Grand Rapids: Fleming H. Revell, 1957, p. vii.

June 12

"Prayer is man's effort to establish contact with God. At its best it is his reverent but intimate communion with God. God is infinite. Man is finite."

> **Albert Edward Day**, *An Autobiography of Prayer*. New York: Harper & Brothers Publishers, 1952, p. 13.

June 13

"Prayer is more than asking; prayer is *taking*. Prayer is more than pleading; prayer is *believing*. Prayer is more than words uttered; it is *an attitude maintained*. How many times we ought to be praying! . . . Prayer is that expression of dependence which lays hold of God's resources – for any need,"

> **Ray C. Stedman**, *Jesus Teaches on Prayer*. Waco: Word Books, Publisher, 1975, p. 35.

June 14

"We, like the disciples, have such a limited conception of prayer. We have said prayers, we have listened to prayers being said in church, we have cried out for help when in trouble, perhaps we have sometimes thanked God. But when we live with Jesus and see him at prayer as the disciples did, we begin to realize that we know very little about prayer and we join with the disciples in saying, 'Lord, teach us to pray.'"

> **Constance Garrett**, *Growth in Prayer*. New York: The MacMillian Company, 1949, p. 4.

June 15

"Prayer is a very strange activity. It is an attempt to communicate with a Being who is not accessible to our ordinary senses. We cannot see, hear, touch, or taste God. We cannot know God in the same way we know another person. And yet we believe in God. We believe God is real; we believe God is personal in the sense that we *can* communicate with God and God with us."

> Evan Pilkington, *Paths to Personal Prayer*. Mystic, CT: Twenty-Third Publications, 1988, p. 14.

June 16

"Not only do we pray too little, but we pray too late. We make the grave mistake of keeping our problems within ourselves, on the pretext that we do not want to 'bother' the Father with our insignificant concerns. We think we ought to wait until something 'really big' comes along. This is not the way of Jesus. When we look to the prayer life of Jesus, we find him demonstrating how vitally important it is to pray at the thresholds of life."

> Vernon R. Schreiber, *Abba: Father*! Minneapolis: Augsburg Publishing House, 1988, p. 11.

June 17

"A fundamental truth in prayer is the sufficiency of the Word of God, along with the enlightening work of the Holy Spirit. This must be the foundation of one's prayer life. And when this is coupled with both the external and internal preparations, it will lead to quality time with our Lord."

> Richard A. Burr with Arnold R. Fleagle, *Developing your Secret Closet of Prayer*. Camp Hill, PA; Christian Publications, 1998, p. 76.

June 18

"The secret of the victorious march of the Early Church across the Roman world is found in its belief in and practice of prayer . . . These early Christians were spiritual conductors, and God manifested himself mightily in their lives . . . The need of the hour in our churches is more prayer . . . that they may become a pulsating, dynamic, spiritual power."

> John Sutherland Bonnell, *The Practice and Power of Prayer*. Philadelphia: The Westminster Press, 1954, p. 46.

June 19

"Prayer is personal communion and dialogue with the living God. Seen from a biblical perspective, prayer is an opportunity and a privilege rather than a burden or a duty. It is the meeting place where we draw near to God to receive his grace, to release our burdens and fears, and to be honest with the Lord."

Kenneth Boa, *Conformed to His Image*. Grand Rapids: Zondervan, 2001. p. 83.

June 20

"Prayer is a place where we can ask all our whys. We must not demand that our whys be answered, but we can ask them out loud and know that God feels our pain. The Bible tells us that God enters into the agony of his people . . . He wants to tell us what he knows we can bear. I only know that when I bring my whys to him in worship, I leave the throne room without them."

Jill Briscoe, *Prayer that Works*. Wheaton: Tyndale House Publishers, 2000, p. 49.

June 21

"Even though we ourselves may not always grasp the intent and goal of our sighings and groanings, we may be assured that they are heard by God so long as we cast ourselves on his mercy . . . Wordless prayer is present not only when we groan in the Spirit or give utterance to our need through cries and sobs: it is also evident when we shout and sing in praise and jubilation"

Donald G. Bloesch, *The Struggle of Prayer*. Colorado Springs: Helmers & Howard Publishers, Inc., 1988, pp. 51-52.

June 22

"Prayer is not an activity that bypasses the mind. There are aspects of prayer that go beyond our understanding, but understanding the truth is essential to all parts of the Christian life, including prayer . . . We are concerned about the will of God when we pray; we come to know the will of God when we are transformed by the renewing of our minds (Romans 12:2)."

Wayne R. Spear, *Talking to God*. Pittsburg: Crown & Covenant Publications, 2002, pp. 9-10.

June 23

"The privilege of prayer is often taken for granted. Most of us would consider it a marvelous honour to be invited to spend an evening in the company of some notable person . . . Yet how significant is such an honour in comparison with the privilege a talking personally to the Lord of glory! To go to him, knowing that he hears and responds to our prayers is, when we consider it, an unbelievable opportunity."

> **John Thornbury**, *Help us to Pray.* Durham, England: Evangelical Press, 1991, p. 17.

June 24

"Imitate no one in your prayers for God's full joy. He himself will direct your petitions as surely as he generates an appetite for himself . . . God in his sovereignty has quite enough power to shape the desires of your heart."

> **Donals E. Demaray**, *How Are You Praying?* Grand Rapids: Francis Asbury Press, 1985, p. 148.

June 25

"As Christians, we know that we can freely share our needs, fears, and joys with a God who truly listens. We also know from His Word, the Bible, that He answers us in His own way. As a spiritual discipline, prayer is on the level of importance of studying God's Word, and we are reminded to pray without ceasing."

> **Henry Thornton**, *Devotional Prayers.* Chicago: Moody Press, 1993, p. 7.

June 26

"Prayer can feel like a lonely experience. Although some prayers are said in groups, before a meal, during worship, or before a meeting at church, prayer is often individual and private. We pray about our worries, fears, joys, needs, and wants. Such prayers are spontaneous, informal, unrehearsed thoughts brought to God."

> **Andrew E. Steinmann**, *Is God Listening*? Saint Louis: Concordia Publishing House, 2004, p. 11.

June 27

"It is to us the most normal thing in the world to discover that Christ devoted much time to teaching an adequate doctrine of prayer to His disciples . . . He gave Himself so utterly to prayer that it was inevitable that He should give it a central place in His message. It was necessary also that the twelve should be instructed in it because of their significance for the Church. After twenty centuries of Christian experience prayer is still supremely important."

> **James G.S.S. Thompson**, *The Praying Christ*. Grand Rapids: Wm. B. Eerdmans Publishing Company, 1959, p. 11.

June 28

"There is a prayer nowhere found among the prayers of our great Exemplar, though it abounds among the prayers of his followers, and should abound yet more. It is the Prayer of Confession . . . He had nothing to confess."

> **John Henry Strong**, *Jesus The Man of Prayer*. Philadelphia – Los Angeles – Chicago: The Judson Press, 1945, p. 105.

June 29

"God is not distant and removed. He is interested in every person. And He cares what happens to them. According to the Bible, man does not have to run a long journey in an effort to find God. Instead, God is seeking men. So, all a man has to do is stand sill and invite God to have fellowship with him."

> **John W. Tresch**, *A Prayer for all Seasons*. Nashville: Broadman Press, 1971, p. 90.

June 30

"The life of Christian praying is a life-long work of love – love for God and Christian love for our fellow men. Praying is no momentary remedy for our spiritual ills and needs. Only as we learn to persevere through thick and thin and down to the end will we reap the rich harvest of Christian prayer."

> **Charles Francis Whiston**, *Teach us to Pray*. Boston: The Pilgrim Press, 1949, p. 189.

JULY

July 1

"When we pray, we pray with our whole selves. We cannot enter into quiet, expectant waiting in the presence of God while our muscles are tense and our nerves tingle with a multitude of reactions set off by our own activities or the stimuli that bombard us from without . . . The first step toward gathering ourselves to an inward quiet will be the releasing of the body from these muscular and organic tensions which so closely affect our mental and emotional states."

> **John L. Casteel**, *Rediscovering Prayer*. New York: Association Press, 1955, p. 136.

July 2

"I have not, then, come to prayer to gain divine power for doing worldly tasks, or for realizing worldly ends. I am come to open the way for heaven's ideals, conditions, qualities, purposes, blessings to flow down into the earth. I came not to harness the power of heaven to the machinery of my earthy plans, but to open the door of heaven for godliness to come down."

> **William Owen Carver**, *Thou When Thou Prayest*. Nashville: Sunday School Board of the Southern Baptist Convention, 1928, p. 38.

July 3

"Desirable, then, as solitude and quiet may be for prayer, they are not essentials. The stillness we look for is an inward stillness that can occupy the centre of our lives, even while a storm rages around us."

> **Richard Bewes**, *Talking About Prayer*. Downers Grove: Inter-Varsity Press, 1979, p. 47.

July 4

"The intercessor makes one of the most daring assumptions ever entertained by the mind of man. He dares to believe that one individual, or a small intercessory group among three billion people on this planet can offer a petition of prayer to the creator and sustainer of all the universe and that their cries will make a difference to God and others."

> **Thomas Albert Carruth**, *Prayer: A Christian Ministry*. Nashville: Tidings, 1971, p. 30.

July 5

"It is far easier to read a book about prayer than it is to pray . . . Books on prayer can give you long lists of helpful suggestions and maybe even some rules of thumb to follow. Yet you know from personal experience that your prayer life has to have more to it than simply following someone else's suggestions or rules. Prayer has to reflect you, involve you, and express your needs."

> **Dale S. Bringman and Frank W. Klos**, *Prayer and the Devotional Life*. Philadelphia: Lutheran Church Press, 1964, p.37.

July 6

"Through prayer, we seek to relate our lives to the activity of God in the world. We express our desires and needs and *at the same time* listen to the call of God for our lives and communities."

> **Jack. L. Seymore**, *Prying the Gospel of Mark*. Nashville: Upper Room Books, 1988, p. 64.

July 7

"Prayer is God and man uniting purposes to accomplish results. Our asking and expecting joined with God's doing bring about results that otherwise would not come to pass."

> **Carolyn Shealy Self & William L**, Self, *Learning to Pray*. Waco: Word Books, 1978, p. 32.

July 8

"Since all the good things that we experience are gifts of God, we may both ask and thank God for things that are good for us in our physical being, but we must view them in their place within the larger purpose of God for our lives."

Terrance Tiessen, *Providence & Prayer*. Downers Grove: InterVarsity Press, 2000, p. 303.

July 9

"What is the secret behind effective prayer? It is the use of the authority entrusted to the believer . . . Prayer is something that happens on this side of heaven only. It is something for which man is expected to take initiative. Man pleads, God gives. Man knocks, God opens. Man asks, God answers. The initiative rests with man."

Ed Silvoso, *That None Should Perish: How to Reach Entire Cities for Christ Through Prayer Evangelism*. Ventura, CA: Regal Books, 1994, p. 194.

July 10

"If we approach God at all, it is with our tails tucked and our fingers crossed. Or we pray with a 'lottery attitude' – maybe we will win, but probably not. The odds are not in our favor. We reason that prayer only works for really 'holy' people. We feel unworthy, unqualified, and undeserving. 'Prayer? Maybe for some, but not for me.' Our feeling of guilt and inadequacy leave us spiritually paralyzed, robbing us of the most precious privilege we have as Christians – communicating with God. Ultimately, we do not pray, or we pray tiny little prayers with great hesitation, because we are afraid."

Terry Teykl, *How to Pray After you've Kicked the Dog*. Muncie, IN: Prayer Point Press, 1999, p. 13.

July 11

"Our proud assertions that God does not demand a fixed hour for prayer are valid, but too often a lack of discipline results in failure to pray at all."

G. Ernest Thomas, *Personal Power through Spiritual Disciplines*. New York - Nashville: Abingdon Press, 1960, p. 65.

July 12

"Probably the biggest secret anyone could share on prayer is just to learn to 'abide' in Christ and then see what happens to your prayer life."

Francis E. Gardner, *Hot Line to Heaven.* Anderson, IN: The
Warner Press, 1970, p. 95.

July 13

"If it were not for sin, our prayers would only consist of praise, adoration,
worship and thanksgiving. There would be no need to deal with . . .
confession."

Richard A. Burr, *Developing your Secret Closet of Prayer.* Camp
Hill, PA: Christian Publications, 1998, p. 121.

July 14

"True prayer starts in the heart of God. He then, through the Holy Spirit,
communicates this to our heart. We feel a need to pray for what he has
communicated – often even thinking that what we are praying for originated
in our own heart and mind. Then we pray back to the Father through the name
of the Lord Jesus and the right He gives us to access the Father in prayer, thus
completing the circle of prayer. As the Father hears our prayer, He then
answers it, since we are praying according to His will."

Glen martin & Dian Ginter, *Drawing Closer.* Nashville: Broadman
& Holman Publishers, 1995, p. 15.

July 15

"We need to be in touch with God for many different reasons: for help when
our strength fails, for comfort in times of pain, for direction when we don't
know which way to turn, for someone to talk to when we are lonely, for
courage to keep on trying when everything is going wrong – and yes, yes! for
those wonderful times when something works out right and we want to share
how deliriously happy we are. And for those almost breathless moments
when we are so filled with thanksgiving that our words come pouring out one
on top of the other – or when we can't get them out at all and we simply pray
with our feelings, knowing that God will understand."

Phyllis Hobe, *The Guideposts Handbook of Prayer.* Carmel, NY:
Guidepost Associates, Inc., 1982, p. 15.

July 16

"To pray, to give thanks and praise to God, who has given us everything and without whom we are nothing, it the most natural act in the world. To be able to pray with other members of the faith community Sunday by Sunday is an awesome privilege."

> **David Sparks**, *Prayers to Share*. Kelowna, B.C. Canada: Wood Lake Books, Inc., 2004, p.7.

July 17

"The purpose of prayer is very simple: to afford a time and a place to be with God because we are his creatures and we need him, and, because love in interdependent and he needs us."

> **J. Moulton Thomas**, *Prayer Power*. Waco: Word Books Publisher, 1976, p. 43

July 18

"At some time in our lives we will all face trouble, illness, fear, death. Few of us at such times are so proud or unbelieving that we do not resort to prayer. We experience a great need for reassurance, to know that someone is on our side to give comfort, endurance, courage – the power to see it through. Perhaps in such moments we are unable to visualize God; however, with few exceptions, we do turn to him - many –of us in despair, some of us in hope and expectation. But if 'the meaning of life is a relationship with Jesus,' it is important to experience *him* in prayer."

> **Helen S. Shoemaker**, *Prayer & Evangelism*. Waco: Word Books Publisher, 1974, p. 39.

July 19

"All prayer is in response to God's prior activity. If it were not for his creative love brooding over his creatures, no 'upward reach' would stir within our hearts. Prayer makes no sense at all unless the pray-er has within his heart the deep conviction of the reality of a personal God."

> **Florence M. Taylor**, *From Everlasting to Everlasting: Promises and Prayers Selected from the Bible*. New York: The Seabury Press, 1973, p. 38.

July 20

"Prayer is fundamental in the Kingdom of God. It is not an optional extra, nor is it a last resort when all other methods have failed. Prayerlessness is a sin; without prayer God's plan for the world cannot be achieved. We do not just pray for the work; prayer is the work. Prayer lifts Christian activities from the realm of human effort to the divine . . . Through prayer we become co-workers with the Lord God Almighty."

> **Patrick Johnstone**, *Operation World: The Day-to-Day Guide to Praying for the World.* Grand Rapids: Zondervan Publishing House, 1993, p. 11.

July 21

"Meditation and contemplation are just the beginnings of the Christian life of prayer. They should lead to a living faith, to a lived experience of God."

> **Thomas H. Green**, *When the Well Runs Dry: Prayer Beyond the Beginnings.* Notre Dame, IN: Ave Maria Press, 1979, p.41.

July 22

"One of the greatest mistakes we make is in trying to get God to answer prayer that is not in the best interest of everyone concerned. For God to completely and continually answer one person's selfish prayers would set him up higher than God."

> **Roy H. Hicks**, *Praying Beyond God's Ability.* Tulsa: Harrison House, 1982, pp. 8-9.

July 23

"There is a sureness, a quietness that results from prayer. When a man knows in his heart that he is proceeding as God directs, his dealings are conducted with a deep sense of harmony and peace. Prayer makes available the power of God. Prayer has an awesome force, for it is always answered. We cannot tell how nor when that answer will come, but come it will, if we keep in tune with divine harmonies."

> **Alexander Lake**, *Your Prayers are Always Answered.* New York: Gilbert Press, Inc, 1956, p. 53.

July 24

"The example of Scripture and the testimony of Christians through the centuries confirm prayer as a means of grace. In prayer we develop our relationship with God, we learn His expectations for our lives, and we receive power and direction. Serious Christians devote themselves to prayer."

> **Rick Melick**, *Called to Be Holy.* Nashville: LifeWay Press, 2001, p. 110.

July 25

"A vibrant prayer life flows from a relationship with the Creator God. His enemy Satan, seeks to confuse and distort the biblical facts about prayer. Believers must be careful to focus on biblical prayer . . . God has taken the initiative with His creation to communicate with Him though prayer."

> **C. Thomas Wright**, *Pray Timer.* Alpharetta, GA: North American Mission Board of the Southern Baptist Convention, 2001, p. 16.

July 26

"Mature prayer thinks of itself as praying with an old and battered blank check. Even though each payment increases its debt, it keeps pushing its dogeared mite forward. For it knows dimly, but adequately, that progress is deeper indebtedness."

> **John Cormody**, *Maturing a Christian Conscience.* Nashville: Upper Room Books, 1985.

July 27

"We have all that in our very natures which works violently against God, God's mind, God's will. How much the more necessary then is it for us to have a prayer life, by which the Spirit is given an opportunity of keeping us straight, keeping us on the line of Divine purpose, keeping us in the ways of the Lord, and in the times of the Lord."

> **T. Austin Sparks**, *The School of Christ.* London, 1964, p. 85.

July 28

"The New Testament prayer meeting reveals the master plan of Jesus. The last thing Jesus did on earth was to build that prayer meeting, and it is the only thing He left behind on planet Earth when He ascended to heaven."

> **Fred Hartley**, *Everything by Prayer*. Camp Hill, PA: Christian Publications, 2003, p. 13.

July 29

"When you are surrounded by the enemy, cry out to the Lord. Since the enemy will always surround you while you live on this earth, prayer – the means of communicating with the one in control – will become a constant necessity. Can I encourage you to cry out and keep on crying out?"

> **Jill Briscoe**, *Prayer that Works*, Wheaton: Tyndale House Publishers, Inc., 2000, p. 186.

July 30

"Prayer unites puny man to Almighty God in miraculous partnership. It is the most noble and most essential ministry God gives to His children – but is the most neglected."

> **P. J. Johnson**, *Operation World: A Handbook for World Intercession*. Bromley, Kent, England: STL Publications, 1978, p. 15.

July 31

"Believers have the high privilege of working with God through intercessory prayer. This privilege is grounded in the divinely ordained nature of prayer."

> **D. Edmond Hiebert**, *Working with God through Intercessory Prayer*. Greenville, SC: Bob Jones University Press, 1991, p. 1.

AUGUST

August 1

"The divine hand is everywhere to be found, the divine voice always to be heard, and the divine summons constantly to be received and obeyed."

> **Maureena Fritz**, *The Exodus Experience: A Journey in Prayer.* Winona, MN: Saint Mary's Press, 1989, p. 25.

August 2

"Everywhere we met with the utmost friendliness, and before our month's visit was ended, we had the joy of seeing some of the leading people in the village and district come out boldly for Christ . . . Had I time and space I could go on multiplying cases where the same results have followed when the cross of Christ has been the pivot of all Christian teaching, and prayer has been the source of power."

> **Rosalind Goforth**, *How I Know God Answers Prayer.* Elkhart, IN: Bethel Publishing, n.d., p. 74.

August 3

"God cannot always grant our petitions immediately. Sometimes we are not fitted to receive the gift. Sometimes He says, 'No' in order to give us something far better."

> **An Unknown Christian**, *The Kneeling Christian.* Grand Rapids, Zondervan Publishing House, 1971, p.86.

August 4

"I believe that prayer on the part of God's people is the secret of having a spiritually successful church. A prayer-centered church program gives tone to all the work from the cradle roll to the choir. Prayer makes its presence felt in every realm of church endeavor. It is indispensable. Prayer not only changes THINGS, but thank God, prayer changes PEOPLE."

> **John Huss**, *Paths to Power.* Grand Rapids: Zondervan Publishing House, 1958, p. 19.

August 5

"You can receive many benefits from praying to God. The profits, blessings, and benefits happen because you pray. Your spiritual side seeks the higher power of God. When you meet God in prayer, your first blessing comes from being in His presence. Other blessings occur as you pray. These may begin during your prayer and carry on through the day. Blessings come through answered prayers."

John Hendrix & Ann B. Cannon, *Circle Your World with Prayer*. Nashville: LifeWay Press, 2000, p. 22.

August 6

"It is not surprising to find difficulty in starting to pray. We learn to pray by praying. We understand more clearly the place and purpose of prayer once we have started and an opening has been made. It is a common experience in conducting a conversation or in the writing of a letter to find that there is hesitation and faltering before the opening. There are false starts to be faced and rough drafts attempted before the flow of thoughts finds an opening."

George Simms, *In my Understanding*. Philadelphia: Fortress press, 1982, p. 6.

August 7

"Every morning it is extremely helpful to picture yourself looking forward to actually meeting with the person of Jesus Christ. To imagine Him sitting across the table, grasping your hand or touching you comfortingly upon your shoulder, wiping a tear, smiling warmly, laughing softly, or raising His eyebrows at your suggestions personalizes your appointment with God."

Becky Tirabassi, *Let Prayer Change Your Life*. Nashville – Atlanta – London – Vancouver: Thomas Nelson Publishers, 1990, p. 59.

August 8

"Prayer is at the center of our faith. It is the place where we communicate with our God. On the one hand, it is the most simple of religious acts. On the other hand, it can be a complicated process that raises many questions for us."

Daniel J. Simundson, *Where is God in my Praying?* Minneapolis: Augsburg Publishing House, 1986, p. 13.

August 9

"After one has entered into a private place and had sufficient stimulation for prayer, there must be progress in one's prayer life if it is to be as effective as possible. One should converse with his Heavenly Father in a natural manner.

> **Francis Landrum Tyler**, *Pray Ye.* Nashville: Broadman Press, 1944, pp. 23-24.

August 10

"Life which is overtired and has no leisure and quietness in prayer is unnatural, however common it may be. Often that condition is due to misjudgment of life's purpose and values, to the choice of the temporal rather than the eternal."

> **George S. Stewart**, *The Lower Levels of Prayer.* New York – Nashville: Abingdon-Cokesbury Press, 1940, p. 129.

August 11

"The purpose of prayer is not to get man's will done on earth; the purpose of prayer is to get God's will done on earth. And God's will is done on earth when we pray. This is because the tools for ministry are the Word of God and prayer."

> **Gary E. Tangeman**, *The Disciple Making Church in the 21st Century.* Fort Washington, PA: Christian Literature Crusade, 1996, p. 180.

August 12

"Prayer is that which makes it possible for God to change his mind without being in the least inconsistent. It is his favorite method of reigning in difficult and distressing situations. Only a sovereign God can inspire prayer and only a sovereign God can answer it. A man's concept of God, therefore, determines the depth of his prayer life. Real prayer begins and ends with God enthroned."

Ralph A. Herring, *The Cycle of Prayer.* Nashville: Broadman Press, 1966, p. 25.

August 13

"If your growth and development depend on your relationship to God, then certainly your effectiveness as a testimony for Him depends on your prayer life. As the Word of God is the source of power, prayer could be considered the channel for power."

LeRoy Eims, *What Every Christian Should Know About Growing.* Wheaton: Victor Books, 1977, p. 37.

August 14

"All prayer is an approach to the throne of God. The rule of God over the affairs of His grace family is from His throne of grace. Part of His purpose is that we reign or rule together with Him; therefore, we are active in the concerns of the throne of God and have access to that throne . . . As we exercise this gift-right of access, we should do so with confident boldness, open sincerity and daring faith."

Marion G. (Bud) Fray, *It is Enough.* Columbus, GA: Brentwood Christian Press, 2000, pp. 29-30.

August 15

"Intercessory prayer is doubly blessed. It blesses him who prays. Its unfailing answer is that he meets with God. In addition, it enlarges his heart, quickens his compassion, and makes him more Godlike. In the second place, it blesses him for whom he prays."

John Sutherland Bonnell, *The Practice and Power of Prayer.* Philadelphia: The Westminster Press, 1954, p. 55.

August 16

"Prayer is more than ordering from the menu of divinity, as if God is some cosmic waiter who serves us at our convenience."

James Melvin Washington, Editor, *Conversations with God.* New York: HarperCollins Publishers, Inc., 1995, p. xxxiv.

August 17

"Christian prayer is always a response to a presence already felt. The awareness of a desire to pray again is already a prayer. As the desert fathers so often said, 'If you want to pray, you are already praying.'"

> **Edward Ferrell**, *Gathering the Fragments.* Notre Dame, IN: Ave Maria Press, 1987, p. 22.

August 18

"Prayer itself can be a training ground for waiting, for passivity. Of course, there is active prayer, prayer that is giving God our to-do list or prayer that is pouring out our hearts before God. But there is also prayer that is passive, that does nothing except *be* in God's presence."

> **Keith Brasley-Topliffe**, *Surrendering to God.* Brewster, MA: Paraclete Press, 2001, p. 33.

August 19

"Prayer has to have a large place in the life of a child of God, and this is why prayer had such a large place in His life, when He was here. The prayer life of the Lord Jesus is, in a certain realm and sense, the biggest problem that you can face. He is Christ, He is the Son of God, He is under the anointing of the Holy Spirit, and He is without sin in His person, and yet, He must spend all the night in prayer after a heavy and long day's work . . . How much the more necessary then is it for us to have a prayer life."

> **T. Austin-Sparks**, *The School of Christ.* London, 1964, pp. 84-85.

August 20

"Prayer is immeasurably more than a form of spiritual therapy. Far loftier is its purpose than the mere production of a sense of well-bring. Prayer is the will of man rising to a common level with the will of God and rendering its performance possible."

> **R. L. Brandt**, *Praying With Paul.* Grand Rapids: Baker Book House, 1966, p. 63.

August 21

"Praying is the most difficult thing we ever learn to do as Christians. Prayer is hard work. It is trench warfare. Now, you may think praying is easy, even a joy. Indeed this can be true. However, real praying, praying that reaches God and moves His heart to answer, is not easy!"

>**Barry Wood**, *Questions Christians Ask About Prayer and Intercession*. Old Tappan, NJ: Fleming H. Revel Company, 1984, p. 9.

August 22

"If there is progress in understanding prayer in depth, it is by the study of the Bible. If there is any overcoming of 'emotional unreality' in prayer, it is by getting our feet more solidly upon the Word of God."

>**Donals E. Demaray**, *Alive to God through Prayer*. Grand Rapids: Baker Book House, 1965, p. 78.

August 23

"Prayer does not require a great deal of methodology; it is simply conversing with God. But because if its strategic role in the /Christian life, the devil does his utmost to discourage its practice."

>**Walter A. Henrichsen**, *Disciples are Made - not Born*. Wheaton: Victor Books, 1974, p. 102.

August 24

"Our need for prayer, grounded in the very constitution of human nature, is aggravated by the nature of the world in which we live: a world of recurring crisis and peril . . . a world in which our only security is rapidly becoming not a material, but a spiritual, security."

>**Kenneth O. Eaton**, *Men on Their Knees*. New York – Nashville: Abingdon Press, 1956, p. 8.

August 25

"Many people think that prayer's primary purpose is to receive things they want. Not so! The best thing we receive through prayer is not a thing – it is

God. When we pray, we invite the presence and power of God into our minds."

> **Herb Miller**, *Connecting with God*. Nashville: Abingdon Press, 1994, p. 59.

August 26

"Prayer is not a lottery that we have a chance in a million to winning. Prayer is a response to a promise, and God pledges His nature that He will hear and answer our prayers. This is a glorious inspiration to pray."

> **Judson Cornwall**, *Praying the Scriptures*. Orlando: Creation House, 1988. p. 76.

August 27

"Spiritual guidance does not have to be passive or solemn, but it should be prayerful and reverent."

> **Gerald May**, *Care of Mind, Care of Spirit*. San Francisco: Harper Sn Francisco, 1992, pp. 210-211.

August 28

"To find words acceptable to God you don't have to be a polysyllabic genius; nor do you need to speak with the tongues of angels. But you do have to focus your thoughts and then formulate those thoughts into precise words if you are to communicate with God."

> **Dale S. Bringman and Frank W. Klos**, *Prayer and the Devotional Life*. Philadelphia: Lutheran Church Press, 1964, p. 66.

August 29

"Prayer must be at the very heart of the disciple-making process. The importance of regular prayer for specific members of your extended family cannot be overemphasized . . . If this vital sept is overlooked, the chances of ever seeing your extended family member come to Christ and the church are slim."

> **Win Arn and Charles Arn**, *The Master's Plan for Making Disciples*. Pasadena, CA: Church Growth, 1982, p. 93.

August 30

"One sure and subtle barrier to effective prayer is a strained and unresolved relationship with another person. Jesus taught that the Father forgives our sins only as we forgive others."

> **Edward C. Briggs**, *A Pilgrim's Guide to Prayer*. Nashville: Broadman Press, 1987, p. 56.

August 31

"Jesus prayed for His disciples and the unbelieving world when alone with God in solitary places. He prayed for their needs and for their release into God's loving arms. He prayed with His disciples in the Upper Room for their growth in purity, unity and protection from the evil one. Jesus' life was an unfinished symphony of prayer for others.

> **Bruce Demarest**, *SoulGuide*. Colorado Springs: NavPress, 2003, p. 176.

SEPTEMBER

September 1

"Why pray? Because at times it is such a fundamental part of our nature that it is instinctive. Because uniquely it conveys, however haltingly, the deepest concerns and the greatest delights of our life. Because at this primitive, basic level of prayer, if we did not pray, we would not be human."

> **Stephen Oliver**, *Why Pray*? Oxford: Lion Publishing plc, 1993, pp. 15-16.

September 2

"While we may never understand how Jesus intercedes for us, we can believe it and count on it. When we do that, the intercession of Jesus will become a great comfort to us. It will teach us to rest more and more in the love of this unseen, but ever-present, Friend. It will anchor our soul. In more practical terms, Jesus' intercession means we do not hold the ropes of faith alone. When we cannot walk in faith any longer, Jesus' prayers carry us through."

> **Brenda Poinsett**, *When Jesus Prayed.* Nashville: Broadman Press, 1981, p. 78.

September 3

"There is more in the first four Gospels about prayer than there is about the church. There is more in these first four books of the New Testament about prayer than about baptism. Here too you will find more about prayer than about Heaven. Noting the teaching and example of our Lord Jesus concerning prayer you will conclude that its place is in the vanguard of Christian activity."

> **Henry Ostrom**, *The Law of Prayer.* Philadelphia – Chicago: The Praise Publishing Co., 1910, p. 5.

September 4

"God makes it abundantly clear that He releases His power in response to the prayers of His obedient children. For believers, the sovereign God is both our loving Father and our Commander-in-Chief. He commands and is gracious. A strong, spiritually fit Christian warrior is one who is consistently and lovingly obedient to His Commander-in-Chief."

> **Archie Parrish**, *Improve Your Prayer Life*. Atlanta: Serve International, 2002, p. 37.

September 5

"In God's eyes the great object of prayer is the opening or restoring of free communion with Himself in a kingdom of Christ, a life communion which may even, amid our duty and service, become as unconscious as the beating of our heart."

> **P.T. Forsyth**, *The Soul of Prayer*. Grand Rapids: Eerdmans Publishing, 1916, pp. 17-18.

September 6

"Make this rule: never pray unless you really mean it, and even though you may repeat essentially the same prayer or prayers, over and over, put real feeling into them."

> **Harold Sherman**, *How to Use the Power of Prayer*. New York: C & R Anthony, Inc., 1958, p. 52.

September 7

"What gets God's attention are humble hearts breaking over sin, yearning for his nearness, and persevering to pray until his glory dwells in our land."

> **Tom White**, *City-wide Prayer Movements*. Ann Arbor, MI: Servant Publications, 2001, p. 159.

September 8

"The one concern of the devil is, to keep the saints from praying. He fears nothing from prayerless studies, prayerless work, prayerless religion. He laughs at our toil, mocks at our religion, but trembles when we pray."

> **A. Sims**, *Mighty Prevailing Prayer*. Grand Rapids: Zondervan Publishing House, n.d. p. 39.

September 9

"Most people think of prayer as an audible activity which calls for the cessation of all other activities. There can also be an inwardness of prayer which does not interfere with other activities and produces no outward, visible indications that it is taking place. There can be a continual prayer of the heart and mind which does not interrupt our daily routine."

> **Robert V. Dodd**, *Praying the Name of Jesus*. Nashville: Upper Room Books, 1985.

September 10

"Because of our chronic egocentricity we think of ourselves as initiating prayer. We seek after God to gain his attention, to have him come into our presence, to respond to our desires and do our will. We will pray far better if we reverse the roles and think of God as seeking to hold our attention, reveal his will to us, and evoke our response."

> **Charles Francis Whiston**, *Pray: A Study of Distinctively Christian Praying*. Grand Rapids: Wm. B. Eerdmans Publishing Co., 1972, p. 28.

September 11

"If your growth and development depend on your relationship to God, then certainly your effectiveness as a testimony for Him depends on your prayer life. As the Word of God is the source of power, prayer could be considered the channel for power."

> **LeRoy Eims**, *What Every Christian Should Now about Growing*. Wheaton: Victor Books, 1977, p. 37.

September 12

"Praying for your enemies distinguishes the Christian from everyone else. It is appropriate behavior for followers of Jesus."

> **Don M. Aycock**, *Prayer 101*. Nashville: Broadman & Holman, 1998, p. 67.

September 13

"Prayer is power, and it changes things. It doesn't matter how difficult your particular situation may seem. God is your very present help in this time of trouble! You don't have to stand back helplessly and hold your breath . . . You can make a difference through prayer."

> **Eastman Curtis**, *Every Day I Pray for My Teenager*. Lake Mary, FL: Charisma House, 1996, p. 13.

September 14

"The character of a man's God ought to determine the nature of his prayers . . . In terms of today, God is the ideal Person, the One to whom we come for blessings that He alone can bestow. To be worthy of the name, whatever their form, our prayers must be spiritual, and they must be real."

> **Andrew W. Blackwood**, *Leading in Public Prayer*. New York. Nashville: Abingdon Press, 1958, p. 107.

September 15

"Millions of prayers may not be prayers at all. They are wishful thinking. They are selfish demands. They have little or no concern for who God is or what Gad wants. They do such damage they are better left unsaid."

> **Leith Anderson**, *When God Says No*. Minneapolis: Bethany House Publishers, 1996, p. 68.

September 16

There are those who in fact do nothing other than ask God for things when they pray. But many realise that they ought not to spend all their time of prayer in asking God for benefits; they realise that they must also express their admiration and love and gratitude towards Him; that they must also express their sorrow for having offended Him, and their determination to live in the way He wishes."

> **Thomas Worden**, *The Psalms are Christian Prayer*. New York: Sheed & Ward, 1961, p. 1.

September 17

"Prayer is at the very heart of man's decision and response to the divine call. In prayer man both responds to the call to be like God, and he asks God for those things which will assist him in developing the image of God in himself."

  Bill Austin, *How to Get What You Pray For.* Wheaton: Tyndale House Publishers, Inc. 1984, p. 89.

September 18

"The character of a man's God ought to determine the nature of his prayers . . . In terms of today, God is the ideal Person, the One to whom we come for blessings that He alone can bestow. To be worthy of the name, whatever their form, our prayers must be spiritual, and they must be real."

  Andrew W. Blackwood, *Leading in Public Prayer.* New York. Nashville: Abingdon Press, 1958, p. 107.

September 19

"We would be wrong in praying only because we felt that God had spoken to us, and in abandoning prayer because we do not feel that God has spoken to us. We have surrendered ourselves into the hands of our Father . . . Our part now it to place this life constantly before him, loyally and faithfully,"

  A. M. Besnard, *Take a Chance on God: A Guide to Christian Prayer.* Denville, NJ: Dimension books, 1977, pp. 101-102.

September 20

"What God offers us in prayer is an awareness of his presence and his power. Jesus . . . emphasized the importance of communication with God. He took himself to God the Father many times, not because he wanted anything that God could give, but because he supremely wanted God himself. If we want what God has to give more then we want God, we are idolaters."

  Charles A. Trentham, *Daring Discipleship.* Nashville: Convention Press, 1969, pp. 79-80.

September 21

"I have found myself pleading in prayer that God will not judge! Now I realize that this is a pretty stupid way to pray. He has to be what He is – perfectly just."

>**Jill Briscoe**, *Hush! Hush! It's Time to Pray – but How?"* Grand Rapids: Lamplighter Books, 1978, p. 100.

September 22

"If our Lord had to pray for Peter, a man who was with Him twenty-four hours a day, how much more need each pastor and church to cry out to God for the new believers in their midst."

>**Waylon B. Moore**, *New Testament Follow-up*. Grand Rapids: Wm. B. Eerdmans Company, 1963, p. 32.

September 23

"Real prayer grows out of the actual situations in which men find themselves. The Bible, as I hope you have long since discovered, does not deal in vague generalities, or general principles, or philosophic conclusions, but rather with specific events, particular people, concrete circumstances."

>**Kenneth Oxner Eaton**, *Men Who Talked with God*. New York – Nashville: Abingdon Press, 1964, pp. 8-9.

September 24

"God speaks to us through His Word and we speak to Him through prayer. The thing to remember is that there are prayers that move the hand of God and there are prayers that have no effect at all."

>**LeRoy Eims**, *Be the Leader You Were Meant to Be*. Wheaton: Victor Books, 1975, p. 21.

September 25

"Prayer is two-way communication with God. True communication between friends, means listening as well as talking . . . Prayer is not non-stop talking."

>**Eric Fife**, *Prayer: Common Sense and the Bible*. Grand Rapids: Zondervan Publishing House 1976, p. 16.

September 26

"You need an audience before God before you attempt audience with your people. Stand in God's presence before you stand before them. You must prevail before God before you can prevail before them. Not till you have worshiped with the seraphim are you ready to worship with your people. Only when you come from the presence of God can you lead them into the presence of God."

> **Wesley L. Duewel**, *Ablaze For God*. Grand Rapids: Francis Asbury Press, 1989, p. 212.

September 27

"Recognition by the world matters very little . . . the only influence that counts is the influence we have in the secret place of prayer."

> **E. Herman**, *Creative Prayer*. New York – London: Harper & Row Publishers, n.d., p. 174.

September 28

"Prayer is not a scheme whereby we can move God into our lives but rather a spiritual exercise through which we draw ourselves toward God until we are a part of His plan and His purpose. The purpose of prayer is not to give you what you want when you want it but to make you the kind of person God wanted you to be when He put you in this world."

> **Jerry D. Locke**, *Now that You've Believed*. Fort Worth: Lake Worth Baptist Church, 1983, p. 33.

September 29

"Prayers give God ports of entry into human affairs. More intercessors provide more avenues for God to work. As we intercede in prayer, we can call forth God's action anywhere."

> **Ben Jennings**, *The Arena of Prayer*. Orlando: NewLife Publications, 1999, p. 25.

September 30

"Prayer is, first of all, about spending time with God. Simply being together is a necessary part of any growing relationship. Our relationship with God will become stronger as we share our dreams and joys, our burdens and our pain, our frustrations and our celebrations. Our dependence on God will become a reality as we express that continuing dependence in prayer."

Douglas A. Kamstra, *The Praying Church Idea Book*, Grand Rapids: Faith Alive Christian Resources, 2001, p. 17.

OCTOBER

October 1

"Lukewarmness in prayer, as in everything else, is nauseating to God, and comes away empty-handed. On the other hand, shameless persistence, the importunity that will not be denied, returns with the answer in its hands."

> **J. Oswald Sanders**, *Prayer Power Unlimited*. Chicago: Moody Press, 1977, pp. 80-81.

October 2

"Learning to enter into complete agreement with God in all things is the most important task a believer faces. Praising God is robbed of meaning if you disagree with Him ... All religious acts are deprived of spiritual significance when unbelief manifests itself in disagreement with God."

> **Richard Owen Roberts**, *Lord, I Agree*. Wheaton: International Awakening Press, 1990, p. 6.

October 3

"When we fervently intercede on behalf of unbelievers with respect and thankfulness, we are identifying with God's very interests and involvement in the salvation process. We are aligning ourselves with God's purpose."

> **R.A. Torrey**, *The Place of Prayer in Evangelism*. Grand Rapids: Baker Book House, 1917, p. 51.

October 4

"The lost are helpless to change the course of their eternal destiny. Without the work of God's Spirit and the witness of the Word, they will remain lost. Believers need to join God's redemptive work through prayer and evangelistic witness for this to be different. As God's people pray for the lost, His Spirit draws them to understand their need for repentance and faith.

> **J. Chris Schofield**, *Praying Your Friends to Christ: Developing a Life of Evangelistic Prayer*. Cary, NC: Baptist State Convention of North Carolina, n.d., p. 20.

October 5

"God desires that we commune daily with him as our heavenly Father. He delights to commune with us, as well as shower us with good things from his storehouse. Daily prayer demonstrates that we are conscious that every present blessing is from God and our dependence in him alone for any future blessing. You cannot be *praying* and be *self-sufficient* at the same time; likewise, it is simply impossible to *neglect prayer* without being *self-reliant*."

> **John G. Reisinger**, *The Sovereignty of God and Prayer*. Frederick, MD: New Covenant Media, 2002, p. 46.

October 6

"There is only one basic rule for prayers alone: Make sure you are left alone. Once this is assured, it will be quite easy to find your own expression of whatever it is that fills your heart at that time. But being left alone in prayer is not as easy as one might think . . . We have a right and a duty to insist: Concerning my prayers alone, leave me alone."

> **David Steindl-Rast**, *Gratefulness, the Heart of Prayer.* New York: Paulist Press, 1984, p. 53.

October 7

"Prayer is a strange genre. It is part poetry, part-association and part love letter to God. When spoken, it is the most intimate, sacred speech we utter. When written down. It becomes a diary of the heart, a journal of our innermost feelings, fears, hopes, desires. It is a full disclosure of a person's thoughts, values, faith – a complete confession."

> **Gary R. Weaver**, *Gentle Words in a Raging Storm*; *Prayers for all Occasions*. Lima, OH: C.S.S. Publishing Company, Inc., 1991, p. 13.

October 8

"In all matters of prayer it is wise to turn with the early disciples to the only one who can 'Teach us to pray' (Luke 11:1). Jesus is enrolling his church afresh in the school of prayer. Churches of many streams and cities have much to gain and much to give as we literally walk together with Jesus."

Graham Kendrick and Steve Hawthorne, *Prayer-Walking: Praying on Site with Insight.* Lake Mary, FL: Charisma House, 1993, p. 16.

October 9

"Prayer is one of the most important aspects of building disciples. If we are to help people grow in their knowledge of Jesus Christ we must pray. In fact, if we do everything else right, but fail to pray, nothing significant will happen."

Carl Wilson, *With Christ in the School of Disciple Building.* Grand Rapids: Zondervan Publishing House, 1976, p. 223.

October 10

"God has made gravity a law in one realm, he has made prayer a law in a higher realm, and it is even greater folly to ignore the latter than the former."

William Patton, *Prayer and its Remarkable Answers.* Chicago: J.S. Goodman, 1876, p. 56.

October 11

"Prayer is communication. We talk *with* God. Not just to him. God talks *with* us too, causing a circle to be whole and closed between us."

Walter Wangerin, Jr., *Whole Prayer: Speaking and Listening to God.* Grand Rapids: Zondervan Publishing House, 1998, p. 29.

October 12

"We partner with God in prayer – it is a process in which we play a very active role. Along the way, God mentors us to enhance all aspects of our prayer life."

Klaus Issler, *Wasting Time with God.* Downers Grove: InterVarsity Press, 2001, p. 219.

October 13

"The habit of prayer implies a certain attitude to life. It predicates God and recognizes His sovereignty over all. It submits all things to His will, rehearses all things in His presence, judges all things by His standard of values, and lives by faith in Him. Prayer is the essence and test of the godly life."

    Samuel Chadwick, *The Path of Prayer*. London: Hodder and Stoughton, 1931, p. 63.

October 14

"Prayer is basic to our spiritual survival. To stay spiritually healthy, we cannot afford to classify prayer as a low priority item. By discovering new insights about it from God's Word, we will not forget its importance."

    John A. Huffman, Jr. *Forgive us our Prayers*. Wheaton: Victor Books, 1980, p. 6.

October 15

"If it is a fact that I must pray, and shall pray when "cornered" by circumstances, then the better I pray the better for me—let me master the practice while there is leisure and time, remembering that here as elsewhere only practice makes perfect."

    Albert D. Belden, *The Practice of Prayer*. New York: Harper & Brothers, 1954, p. 14.

October 16

"Prayer is our Declaration of Dependence on God, a declaration that needs constant affirmation. Our greatest personal need is simultaneously our toughest problem – depending on God. Since the beginning, we mortals have fought this sense of dependence and defied God's orders. Many have been tempted to live as though there were no God or as though he exists for our benefit. The command to pray is a reminder that we cannot live without God's power, love and guidance."

    David Allan Hubbard, *The Practice of Prayer*. Downers Grove: InterVarsity Press, 1972, p. 13.

October 17

"As you develop in prayer, you will start to see growth. This will come as you begin to reach out beyond yourself and your family and broaden your self-centered praying to include a wider scope of requests."

Glen Martin and Dian Ginter, *Power House*. Nashville: Broadman & Holman Publishers, 1994, p. 99.

October 18

"In the record of beginnings, and in the 'occasional correspondence' of the Apostolic Church, covering a multitude of topics and of situations, prayer is referred to no less than one hundred and eighty times – about once in every twenty-three verses. The early Christians could not discuss their work or share their experiences without the words of prayer being continually upon their lips."

Reginald E.O. White, *Prayer Is the Secret*. New York: Harper & Brothers Publishers, 1958, pp. 13-14.

October 19

"Prayer presents the greatest opportunity for soul-winning, and there is precious reward promised to those who bring souls to Christ."

Lewis Sperry Chafer, *True Evangelism: Winning Souls Through Prayer*. Grand Rapids: Kregel Publications, 1993, p. 69.

October 20

"Given the example of Christ's continual prayer life, why do we spend so little time in prayer? Jesus constantly went off by himself to pray, and at times spent the entire night in prayer. Why then do we pray so infrequently?"

Richard C. Meyer, *One Anothering*. Philadelphia: Innisfree Press, 1990, p. 27.

October 21

"Sometimes I really want the will of God – and sometimes I don't. When His will goes against mine, I balk. If I pause long enough, I realize that if I'm serious about my faith, I really do want His will. Just what am I praying for when I say *Thy will be done*? . . . Great things are possible if we yield ourselves to God's will and make this our highest ambition.

John A. Huffman, *Forgive Us Our Prayers*. Wheaton, IL: Victor Books, 1980, p. 29

October 22

"Prayer is welcoming our Father's presence into a lifetime conversation with our hearts. Calling Him up throughout the hour, day, week, month, year of our lives like calling up your best friend, or your father or mother, or the person you love most in the world. Finally, prayer is our ultimate conversation of knowing and being known, of loving and being loved. This communion with our Father sustains us for this lifetime and whets our appetites for the next."

> **Dudley J. Delffs**, *The Prayer Centered Life*. Colorado Springs: NavPress, 1997, p. 186.

October 23

"We are always in the presence of God. If we live each moment conscious of His presence, we shall not have to readjust our mental attitude when we begin to pray, but we shall pray to the One we have been silently including in our every thought and conversation."

> **Dorothy C. Haskin**, *A Practical Primer on Prayer*. Chicago: Moody Press, 1951, pp. 14-15.

October 24

"The early understanding of Christian prayer is an activity by which a disciple of the Lord, with him and through him, seeks God in faith, intercedes with God in hope, experiences and communes with God in love and filled with the Spirit of Jesus, reaches out in concern and service to others."

> **Agnes Cunningham**, *Prayer: Personal and Liturgical*, Wilmington, DL: Michael Glazier, 1985, p. 31.

October 25

"Prayer is not an assortment of chosen words or expressions, not a repetition of certain prescribed forms, but it is the cry of the human soul that comes from the heart of the praying one. Prayer is communication with God; in it man lays his inmost being open before God, presents his need, puts down the burden of his soul which he is unable to bear at the feet of the Most High."

> **N. I. Saloff-Astakhoff**, *The Secret and Power of Prayer*. Chicago: Good News Publishers, 1948, pp. 58-59.

October 26

"Christian prayer is both private and public, but it is not exclusively either of these. It is deeply personal, but it is not individualistic. It will invariably assume corporate expression, but the personal element is never missing in true prayer."

> **Donald G. Bloesch**, *The Struggle of Prayer*. Colorado Springs: Helmers & Howard Publishing, Inc, 1988, p. 40.

October 27

"Prayer is a paradox and a mystery. It can be the simplest and easiest experience of life – like enjoyment of a sunset in the late summer evening, the unexpected smile of a child; or it can be the most anguishing moment of a lifetime – to say yes in the face of death or tragedy."

> **Edward J. Farrell**, *Gathering the Fragments*. Notre Dame, IN: Ave Maria Press, 1987, p. 19.

October 28

"Prayer is the perennial privilege of the children of God and should not be neglected for a single day . . . No one ever comes to know the highest joy and power of prayer until he becomes constant in it practice."

> **J. Paul Carleton**, *Rejoicing in Prayer*. Shawnee, OK: Oklahoma Baptist University Press, 1949, pp. 45-46.

October 29

"Those who persevere in the labor and travail of prayer will know hours of unexpected joy, in which the renewing love of God moves in and buoys them up to new levels of living peace such as they can hardly anticipate,"

> **John L. Casteel**, *Rediscovering Prayer*. New York: Association Press, 1955, p. 228.

October 30

"Although prayer is an intensely personal matter, it is not individualistic. It is . . . an expression of 'community,' of human solidarity, of spiritual fellowship within the body of Christ."

Olive Wyon, *The School of Prayer*. Philadelphia: The Westminster Press, 1944, p. 12.

October 31

"Remember that prayer is simply talking to God and listening for His response. You can talk to Him just as you would talk to someone sitting right next to you. You do not have to use ornate language to talk to Him. You do not even need to worry if your prayer makes sense. God knows the heart, He knows your thoughts; you do not need to explain everything clearly for Him to understand. Coming to God is the important thing.

Jonathan Graf, *The Power of Personal Prayer*. Colorado Springs: NavPress, 2002, p. 32.

NOVEMBER

November 1

"It is my conviction that no single experience provides more spiritual impact upon a life than the act and reality of prayer."

Albert M. Wells, Jr, Compiler, *As Touching the Holy*. Grand Rapids: Baker Book House, 1980, p. 3

November 2

"God is not boring, and prayer to Him should not be dull either. We are given gifts of imagination and creativity that can be used to make prayer more exciting for ourselves and for others with whom we pray."

W. Edward Thiele, *Fruitful Discipleship*. New Orleans: Insight Press, 1994, p. 81.

November 3

"Prayer is guided by right living as well as by right thinking. True prayer means behaving in a way that is worthy of God's company."

James Houston, *Prayer: The Transforming Friendship*. Oxford, England: Lion Publishing pc, 1989, p. 7.

November 4

"The power which is available through prayer is often lost when we assume the attitude of a commander who is summoning God to satisfy his personal desires."

G. Ernest Thomas, *Personal Power through the Spiritual Disciplines*. New York – Nashville: Abingdon Press, 1960, p. 73.

November 5

"Most people think of prayer as a way to contact God. Consequently, regardless of the religious label they attach to themselves, they pray more or less frequently. Instinctively people believe in God, and instinctively they pray to God. Christians, however, have a special interest in prayer. We believe it is a way to contact the true God who has revealed himself in love and who has spoken to us already in his Word, the Bible."

Thomas L. Constable, *Talking to God.* Grand Rapids: Baker books, 1995, p. 15.

November 6

"Secret prayer is such an essentially spiritual duty that the Bible nowhere lays down laws and rules either as to times or as to places for such prayer."

Alexander Whyte, *Lord, Teach Us to Pray.* London: Hodder & Stoughton Limited, 1922, p. 236.

November 7

"Prayer is fellowshipping with the Father – a vital, personal contact with God Who is more than enough. We are to be in constant communion with Him."

Germaine Copeland, *Prayers that Avail Much.* Tulsa, OK: Harrison House, 1989, p. 15.

November 8

"This is what prayer is all about: not what I can get from God, but to have my heart so radically changed by Him that I come to want only what God wants for me."

Richard Burr, *Developing your Secret Closet of Prayer.* Chicago: Wing Spread Publishers, 1998, p. 6.

November 9

"God hears prayers. How exactly remains a mystery. God hears the prayers we speak aloud. God hears the prayers we lift in silence. God even hears when words for prayer escape us, through the Spirit . . . So let us pray, for God does hear."

John Indermark, *Traveling the Prayer Paths of Jesus.* Nashville: Upper Room Books, 2003, p. 59.

November 10

"Prayer is not a performance but an intimate relationship between an individual and God . . . Jesus' insistence that we enter our closets and pray to God secretly is not a literal requirement for effective prayer. Rather, He was emphasizing the fact that prayer is between the individual and God."

> **David L. Jenkins**, *Great Prayers of the Bible*. Nashville Broadman Press, 1990, p. 12.

November 11

"One whose life is spent in fellowship with God will constantly seek and find opportunities for swift and frequently-recurring approaches to the throne of grace."

> **D.M. M'Intyre**, *The Hideen Life of Prayer*. Minneapolis: Bethany Fellowship, Inc., n.d., p. 27

November 12

"Happily, the use of prayer has no adverse accompaniments. Its side effects are all on the plus side. Along with achieving its primary goal, the answer to prayer, it may simultaneously bestow other blessings."

> **Virginia Whitman**, *The Excitement of Answered Prayer*. Grand Rapids: Baker Book House, 1973, p. 97.

November 13

"All true prayer is person-to-Person communion and encounter with God. It involves trustful dependence, gratitude, adoration, confession, petition, openness to God, decision, and love. It includes the sustained desire to understand and do God's will in spite of counteracting impulses."

> **Mack B. Stokes**, *Talking With God*. Nashville: Abingdon Press, 1989, p. 13,

November 14

"In our prayers we often aim at nothing and hit it every time. We expect nothing from God and get precisely that. Much of our praying never goes beyond the ceiling."

> **Eric Fife**, *Prayer Common Sense and the Bible*. Grand Rapids: Zondervan Publishing House, 1976, p. 87

November 15

"When a Christian looks at the map of the world and sees the large areas beyond control or influence of the gospel he cannot refrain from praying for the day when all the men of all the nations shall be turned to him who should rightfully possess them.:

> **Frances Landrum Tyler**, *Pray Ye: A Study of Prayer and Missions*. Nashville: Broadman Press, 1944, p. 18,

November 16

"The only way to completely fail in prayer is to fail to pray!"

> **Sue Curran**, *The Praying Church*. Lake Mary, FL: Creation House Press, 1987, p. 83.

November 17

"At times we do not set ourselves to pray, but turn eagerly to God, even if with stumbling words and confused desires and thoughts. Whether we be driven by love for others or by joy or need or sorrow, these are likely to be times of real communion and response."

> **George S. Stewart**, *The Lower Levels of Prayer*. New York – Nashville: Abingdon-Cokesbury Press, 1939, p. 22.

November 18

"True communion with the Presence is a healthy and life-giving relationship in which we seek God – not an experience, not an emotion, a mood, or a feeling – in which we renounce any test of ecstasy or illumination as evidence."

> **Lance Webb**, *The Art of Personal Prayer*. New York – Nashville: Abingdon Press, 1962, p. 155.

November 19

"We should pray for deliverance, and we should learn to resist the attacks of Satan in the power of Jesus Christ. But we should always pray in an attitude of humble acceptance of that which is God's will. Sometimes God's will is deliverance from the adversity; sometimes it is the provision of grace to accept the adversity. Trusting God for the grace to accept adversity is as much an act of faith as is trusting Him for deliverance from it."

> **Jerry Bridges**, *Trusting God*. Colorado Springs: NavPress, 1988, p. 213.

November 20

"Most Christians, at one time of another in their lives, experience answers to prayer that are nothing less than miraculous. The factors and influences that come together to change a situation, for example, cannot be attributed to coincidence. . . . In order for God's will to be accomplished in a particular situation, He may choose to circumvent normal circumstances, or even His own natural laws."

> **David L. Jenkins**, *Great Prayers of the Bible*. Nashville: Broadman Press, 1990, p. 32.

November 21

"If you're just learning how to pray, start by getting to know the One you pray to. Enjoy your time with him. Be intimate with God when you pray. Prayer isn't reciting words to a distant deity. It's spending enjoyable time with a respected friend."

> **Woodrow Kroll**, *When God Doesn't Answer*. Grand Rapids: Baker Books, 1997, p. 20.

November 22

"Pray with your feelings if they are spontaneously present, pray without them if they are absent, pray in spite of them if they are contrary. If you hoist the sail of your prayer-boat and no wind of feeling is blowing, get out the oars of the will and row. When your prayer is a matter of will your constancy of purpose is itself a costly and precious offering to God."

> **Stephen Winward**, *How to Talk with God*. Wheaton: Harold Shaw Publishers, 1961, p. 98.

November 23

"Unmistakably does our Lord teach that the power of prayer does not depend on a multitude of words. We are not heard for our 'much-speaking.' Nor are we under the necessity of endless explanation and expansion, as though we were dealing with one who is ignorant of our needs, or incapable of understanding our words."

Arthur T. Pierson, *Lessons in the School of Prayer*. St, Louis: Miracle Press, 1971, p. 45.

November 24

"Most Christians do not willfully neglect prayer, yet neither can they claim to do it ignorantly. They are aware of its tremendous possibilities, of the need, of the urgency to pray, yet they fail to pray because they let it be crowded out."

Virginia Whitman, *The Excitement of Answered Prayer*. Grand Rapids: Baker Book House, 1973, p. 121.

November 25

"Prayer should be natural and spontaneous for a human being. After all, God made us to have communication with him. We need that relationship with the one who is everlasting and good because we live in a world that is transient and sometimes evil. God has told us to pray – for our own good."

Daniel J. Simundson, *Where is God in my Praying?* Minneapolis: Augsburg Publishing House, 1986, p. 25.

November 26

"The man after God's own heart in prayer always as a matter of fact builds for himself a little sanctuary, all his own; not to shut God in, but to shut all that is not of God out. He builds a house for God, before he has yet built a house for himself."

Alexander Whyte, *Lord, Teach us to Pray*. London: Hodder & Stoughton Limited, 1922, p. 12.

November 27

"Christians must pray. Praying is not merely something we ought to do, or something we would enjoy doing, or even something that would be helpful. It is essential. It is as essential for the Christian as air, water, and food are for any person."

> **Carl Wilson**, *With Christ in the School of Disciple Building*. Grand Rapids: Zondervan Publishing House, 1976, p. 226.

November 28

"Prayer is the unseen wire stretched from the very heart of God to the heart of man. It is just as real and certain as electricity and gravitation; it is no more mysterious; it is no less practical. It is just as reasonable to expect to accomplish something by this means as by any other law or invention."

> **Courtland Myers**, *Real Prayer*. New York – Toronto: Fleming H. Revell Company, 1911, p. 11.

November 29

"It's okay to tell God how you feel. After all, He already knows. I've never told God anything He didn't already know. I've never heard God gasp in surprise at anything I said. I've never heard God say in response to any confession, 'I would never have believed that of you.'

> **Ronald Dunn**, *When Heaven is Silent*. Nashville: Thomas Nelson Publishers, 1994, p. 131.

November 30

"When you engage in serious conversation with someone you love and trust, your style of conversation is in a manner which is appropriate to your own personality. It does not follow prescribed rules and regulations. It is free expression and moves spontaneously from concern to concern, from one idea to another, without necessarily following an organized pattern. This is the way prayer should be."

> **Erwin Kolb**, *A Prayer Primer*. St. Louis: Concordia Publishing House, 1982, p. 19.

DECEMBER

December 1

"There is no area of the Christian life more susceptible to failure than that of private prayer. And because the prayer is private, the failure also is private, a burden to be carried alone with all its attendant feelings of guilt."

> **Michael Walker**, *Hear me, Lord*. Old Tappan, NJ: Fleming H. Revell Company, 1969, p. 9.

December 2

"Perhaps you think of prayer as wanting something from God when you pray. Up to a point this is right: you want mercy, strength to resist temptation, answers to particular petitions, graces of one sort or another. But it would be more true to say that God wants something out of you when you pray."

> **Dom Hubert van Zeller**, *Prayer in Other Words*. Springfield, IL: Templegate Publishers, 1963, p. 15.

December 3

"This is the difficulty with much of our prayer - it is a spasmodic cry of emergency rather than the habitual fellowship and conversation of a heavenly life. If you were accustomed to walking close by His side, you would not want to get far from Him and have to call loudly in the hour of extremity."

> **A.B. Simpson**, *The Life of Prayer*. Camp Hill, PA: Christian Publications, 1989, pp. 85-86.

December 4

"Go into a church in Asia, Africa, Latin America, Europe, North America – anywhere. You will find far more women than men. And the real prayer warriors, those on the cutting edge of intercessory prayer ministries worldwide, are usually women."

> **Loren Cunningham and David Joel Hamilton**, *Why Not Women?* Seattle: YWAM Publishing, 2000, pp. 16-17.

December 5

"Sometimes we think that the purpose of prayer is to inform God of our needs. We believe he is ignorant of what is going on in our lives, and if we don't tell him, he will never know. We assume he is too busy counting hairs on people's heads to be concerned about our needs."

> **Kent Crockett**, *The 911 Handbook*. Peabody, MA: Hendrickson Publishers, Inc., 1997, p. 4.

December 6

"Affective prayer approaches God through the emotions. This does not imply an emotionalism but a deepened awareness of our feelings. Affective prayer takes account of a range of emotions from 'noticing with interest' to 'love.'"

> **Ben Campbell Johnson**, *To Pray God's Will*. Philadelphia: The Westminster Press, 1987, p. 14.

December 7

Authentic prayer of any kind is the talk of the soul. When one truly prays, one – to use psalm-language – lifts up his soul."

> **Gordon MacDonald**, *The Life God Blesses*. Nashville – Atlanta – London – Vancouver: Thomas Nelson Publishers, 1994, p. 198.

December 8

"Did you realize that one way God measures your life is by your intercession? Your earnest prayer can expand your life beyond any other limits that you can reach. Measure your life by your fervent, prevailing prayer for others and for Christ's kingdom. At testimony time in heaven when people thank you for your prayers, how many will rise to thank God for your prevailing intercession, for the holy influence of your life? Measure the breadth, depth, height, and length of your life by your intercession."

> **Wesley L. Duewel**, *Measure Your Life*. Grand Rapids: Zondervan Publishing House, 1992, p. 63

December 9

"It is not enough to have a clear mental picture when we pray. It must be a picture of what we desire and not one of what we do not want. Prayer is always for and in behalf of a thing or condition to be received, never against."

> **Agnes Sanford**, *Hands of Prayer*. England: Arthur James Limited, 1953, p. 48.

December 10

"The busier we are, the more do we become burdened with responsibilities, and the more do we stand in need of these times when we can renew our contact with God."

> **Paul Tournier**, *Adventure of Living*. New York: Harper & Row, 1976, p. 217.

December 11

"Prayer involves more than just asking for things for ourselves. An important element of prayer is intercession – our prayers for others."

> **Ronald Klug**, *How to Keep a Spiritual Journal*. Minneapolis: Augsburg Books, 1993, p. 84.

December 12

"It would have been matter for surprise if, among manifold subjects on which Jesus gave instruction to His disciples, prayer had not occupied a prominent place. Prayer is a necessity of spiritual life, and all who earnestly try to pray soon feel the need of teaching how to do it."

> **Alexander Balmain Bruce**, *The Training of the Twelve*. New York – London: Harper & Brothers, n.d., p. 52

December 13

"Knowing God requires only that we live. No one alive is ever out of range of God's presence and blessing. Knowing God more deeply, however, requires our willingness to stop, notice, listen, and receive."

> **Kirk Byron Jones**, *Addicted to Hurry*. Valley Forge, PA: Judson Press, 2003, p. 54.

December 14

"Jesus . . . saw prayer as his central task. Looking at his life, we are struck by the time he spent praying, especially given the demands he endured . . . for him, prayer was his first obligation . . . Jesus knew if he did not fall on his knees, he would soon fall on his face."

Richard C. Meyer, *One Anothering, Volume 1.* Philadelphia, PA: Innisfree Press, 1990, pp. 29-30.

December 15

"Petition has as its goal the altering of life situations. The Bible suggests that prayer can work various effects on the one who prays, the one for whom intercession is offered, the spiritual realm, and even God. To this end petition is the laying hold of and the releasing of God's willingness and ability to act in accordance with divine will on behalf of the creation God loves."

Stanley J. Grenz, *Prayer: The Cry for the Kingdom.* Peabody, MA: Hendrickson Publishers, 1988, p. 47.

December 16

"Prayer is either a problem or a power. It is either an enigma to be viewed with suspicion and doubt or an experience that gives quiet certitude and strength to all our living."

Lance Webb, *The Art of Personal Prayer.* New York: Abingdon Press, 1962, p. 5.

December 17

"Did you ever pray when your prayers seemed to bounce off the wallpaper? Have you ever started to pray, but felt you were talking to yourself? Be careful! Just because we may feel God is far off, that we're alone, or that He doesn't hear us when we pray, we can't give in to a false notion of the almighty and omnipresent God. The Bible teaches us that God is everywhere present. We are surrounded by God, whether we acknowledge His presence or not."

Dandi Daley Knorr, *When the Answer is NO.* Nashville: Broadman Press, 1985, p. 25.

December 18

"People who pray out of habit have understood that prayer is so important that they must do it whether they feel like it or not. Habit will tide us over when faith is at a low ebb, which means that it has the added advantage of taking our eyes off ourselves and our passing waves of skepticism."

> **Linette Martin**, *Practical Praying*. Grand Rapids: William B. Eerdmans Publishing Company, 1997, p. 8.

December 19

"When we know the depth of our need for God and when we are convinced that God's purpose is far superior to our preference, then we are ready to yield to God and to do God's will. 'Your will be done' is a prayer that God will bridle us and direct us, wherever that may lead."

> **Brian J. Dodd**, *Praying Jesus' Way*. Downers Grove: InterVarsity Pres, 1997, p. 77.

December 20

"There are at least two things that happen when we pray together than cannot happen when we pray alone. First, when we pray together, our faith in mutually strengthened . . . Second, when we pray together, the joy is multiplied when the answers finally come."

> **Ray Pritchard**, *Beyond All You Could Ask or Think*. Chicago: Moody Publishers, 2004, p. 19.

December 21

"Most people, when they drift away from worship and prayer, do not do so because they have set themselves against God, but because something has not worked out right for them. They have become discouraged. They are troubled. They feel they've lost touch with God. They don't see how they can get things going again. They have given up trying."

> **Vernon R. Schreiber**, *Abba! Father!* Minneapolis: Augsburg Publishing House, 1988, p. 70.

December 22

"Christ's earthly life was one of unceasing prayer. He prayed at His baptism. He prayer before sending out His disciples. He prayed at the grave of Lazarus. He prayed for Peter that his faith might not fail. He prayed on the Mount of Transfiguration. He prayed when they would have made Him King. He prayed at the last supper. He prayed in Gethsemane. He prayed on the cross for His enemies. If Christ, the only sinless man who ever walked the earth, lived a life of constant communion with the Father through prayer, how much must we weak, fleshly, earth-bound mortals need it."

> **James H. McConkey**, *Prayer.* Pittsburg: Silver Publishing Society, 1924, pp. 7-8.

December 23

"We must certainly conclude that there is not place where an individual or a company may be in need of divine help but where it is proper to pray. If the soul be always in the spirit of prayer, so that every breath is a prayer, then everywhere one goes there will be a place of prayer."

> **C. J. Kinne**, *Prayer: The Secret of Power.* Kansas City: Nazarene Publishing House, 1913, p. 36.

December 24

"Many view prayer as a privilege only, but it is also a responsibility. Paul teaches in Colossians 4:12 that prayer is work. We are under a divine mandate to pray. Jesus said, 'Men ought to pray . . .'"

> **Sam Wolfe**, *The Deeper Secrets of Prayer.* Huntsville, AL: Evangel Ministries, 2002, p. x.

December 25

"Let us His make Satan tremble. Let us give ourselves to prayer . . . God is calling His people to prayer in these days. The Bride must be united with her Bridegroom in this marvelous work of intercession."

> **A. Sims**, *Mighty Prevailing Prayer.* Grand Rapids: Zondervan Publishing House, n.d. p. 45.

December 26

"The moment in which we lift up our hearts in prayer to God, in the face of our congregation, should be the supreme moment of inspiration both for them and for us. Our prayer should be at one and the same spontaneous and carefully thought out."

>   **Robert Geffen**, *The Handbook of Public Prayer*. New York – London: The Macmillan Company, 1963, p. vii.

December 27

"Prayer is communication between two lovers. God loves us like no one else loves us. God's care for us reaches infinite proportions, God's interest in us embraces every aspect of our lives, God desires to hear from us regularly and invites us into a running conversation about our thoughts, needs, and concerns."

>   **C. Welton Gaddy**, *A Love Affair with God*. Nashville: Broadman & Holman Publishers, 1995, p. xiv.

December 28

"In all types of prayer we come time and again to the necessity for a deeper commitment and self-offering until the whole of our life and interests is laid upon the altar of God. We discover that a great mystery is to be found in the twofold movement of renunciation and grace. By giving all, we receive all."

>   **John B. Magee**, *Reality and Prayer*. New York: Harper & Brothers, 1957, p. 140.

December 29

"There is nothing on earth that Satan so fears as prayer. He does not know how to cope with prayer, so he concentrates on keeping you from prayer or getting you to give up before you get prayer's answer."

>   **Wesley L. Duewel**, *Mighty Prevailing Prayer*. Grand Rapids: Francis Asbury Press, 1990, p. 233.

December 30

"A heart ready and reliable is the only ground upon which to build a prayer life that shall be persuasive and prevailing. The character of the one who prays always sets a limit upon the answer God can give."

> **Reginald E.O. White**, *They Teach us to Pray*. New York: Harper & Brothers Publishers, 1957, p. 18.

December 31

"Praying is Christ's name is a commitment to waiting on God's timing to put our own plans and agendas at the service of his divine economy. The very term which we have taken from common usage, 'unanswered prayer' is a dubious one. It should be *'not-as-yet-answered-prayer'*"

> **David Willis**, *Daring Prayer*. Atlanta: John Knox Press, 1977, p. 133.

AND FINALLY

No book of prayer quotes would be complete without one from one of my favorite writers, the late Charles Schultz, creator of Peanuts cartoons:

Linus is praying beside his bed when interrupted by Lucy.

He says, "I think I've made a new theological discovery."

"What is it?" inquires Lucy.

Linus replies (holding his praying hands upside down), "If you hold your hands upside down you get the opposite of what you pray for."

I truly hope the quotes in this collection will help you get "what you pray for."